AMERICA'S STUPIDEST BUSINESS DECISIONS

Quill

William Morrow

New York

America's Stupidest Business Decisions

101 Blunders, Flops, and Screwups

Bill Adler, Jr., and Julie Houghton

Illustrations by Loel Barr

It is the policy of William Morrow and Company, Inc., and its imprints and affiliates, recognizing the importance of preserving what has been written, to print the books we publish on acid-free paper, and we exert our best efforts to that end.

Library of Congress Cataloging-in-Publication Data
Adler, Bill, 1956–
    America's stupidest business decisions : 101 blunders, flops, and
  screw ups / by Bill Adler, Jr., and Julie Houghton ; illustrations by
  Loel Barr.—1st ed.
      p.   cm.
  Includes bibliographical references and index.
  ISBN 0-688-15152-3
    1. Consumer goods—United States.   2. Product management—United
  States.   3. Brand name products—United States—Marketing.
  I. Houghton, Julie. II. Title.
  HF1040.8.A35   1997
  338.7'0973—dc21   97-8566
                                            CIP

Printed in the United States of America
First Edition

1 2 3 4 5 6 7 8 9 10

BOOK DESIGN BY CHRIS WELCH

THIS BOOK IS dedicated to those business-men and -women able to keep their heads up and their sense of humor intact as they risk hardship and humiliation in their pursuit of the almighty dollar.

BEFORE WE BEGIN . . .

The American system is a marvel that is admired, envied, and imitated throughout the world. America's large corporations and small businesses, institutions and governments, churn out a world-leading gross domestic product in excess of one trillion dollars annually.

The U.S. is first in innovation and teaches the world how to do business. It has some of the brightest minds and best talents, and is a magnet for people with ideas and ambition from all countries. There is no question that America, and Americans, certainly know how to do things right.

This book is about the other side of the American success coin. Here you will read about our all too human tendency to err. We offer the following recounting of I.Q.-challenged antics in the hope that, through our equally human capacity to laugh at our mistakes, we can all learn from them.

AMERICA'S
STUPIDEST
BUSINESS
DECISIONS

EDISON'S DREAM HOUSE

THOMAS EDISON'S CONCRETE PLANS

O f all the inventors in the world's history, few have had the impact on human life as has Thomas Alva Edison. The list of his achievements is long and lustrous. He is best remembered for the electric light bulb, but the phonograph, motion picture, and countless other inventions were all his.

Still, nobody's perfect, and even the great Thomas Edison sometimes had a brainstorm that turned out to be a dud. Among those, his attempt to popularize the concrete house was probably his worst idea.

In 1908, Edison patented his plans for concrete houses and commissioned a New York architectural firm to design molds for an entire structure including basement, roof, floors, walls, stairs, doorways, baths, pipes, and other infrastructure to be cast in a single piece. It was Edison's hope to use the output of a cement factory he owned to build a vertically integrated business: cement houses from stones to stairwells. The principal attraction of the Edison concrete dwellings was to be their low cost. You could buy a three-story, six-room house for only $1,200, provided that the houses were built in lots of a hundred or more.

Not surprisingly, the Edison process produced a comparatively dull and tiresome structure with little "curb appeal" that even the low price couldn't overcome. Somehow, concrete just didn't have the allure of wood, bricks, or other more traditional building materials. Builders were reluctant to shell out the $175,000 Edison was asking for the molds and equipment to manufacture the structures.

So with no one to build or buy them, Edison's idea of concrete communities more or less sank of its own weight. Nonetheless, Edison's enthusiasm for concrete never waned. He had plans for concrete pianos and refrigerators and even built a few concrete cabinets to house some of his famous phonographs.

Edison's refusal to accept the concrete failure was a signature of his style, and in fact, his doggedness in the face of defeat helped carry him to many of his successes. Among the stories that surround the legendary inventor is the tale that accompanies his quest to create a viable storage battery. It is said that Edison failed in some ten thousand attempts to create the device, but rather than acknowledge failure he is said to have responded: "Why, I have not failed. I've just found ten thousand ways that don't work."

2

FORD'S MOST FAMOUS FLOP

The Ford Motor Company is one of the world's most stunning industrial success stories. From the Model T to the Thunderbird to the Taurus, Ford has a distinguished history of product innovation and success.

It is also the company that produced the auto industry's most famous flop. The car was called the Edsel, and it made its debut for the 1958 model year. In three years of production before the car was discontinued, Ford sold only about a hundred thousand models of the automobile that has come to be synonymous with the word "loser" in American slang. And if you believe that might be an overstatement, consider this: It's been reported that during its brief passage on America's highways, only one Edsel was ever reported stolen.

It was not supposed to have been this way. Edsel, named after company founder Henry Ford's only son, was supposed to have been Ford's answer to increasing market share in the mid-price family sedan class. Too many people were seeing the U.S.A. in their Chevrolets for Ford executives' tastes, and the company set out to build a winning competitor from the ground up.

The Edsel was the most extensively researched new product in American automotive history. No detail was overlooked in the attempt to create a breakthrough sales success. The naming of the car, for instance, involved almost unbelievable effort. Ford's ad agency came up with eight thousand alternative names, but none seemed quite right. A poet was even commissioned to devise other alternatives before the final uninspired choice of name, Edsel, was made.

The driving idea behind the Edsel's birth was to create a new car that fulfilled the American middle-class family's status wishes as well as its needs for transportation. It was probably a good idea, but the execution could not have been worse. Incredibly, there was almost nothing about the Edsel that people liked, and many of its allegedly advanced features were turkeys from the start.

Instead of a gearshift, the Edsel had a push-button transmission mounted in the center of the steering wheel. The positioning of the transmission was innovative, but it could not obscure the inferior performance of the new system. The buttons would often stick, sometimes requiring a pounding with a hammer to get them loose. Electrically operated hoods and trunks refused to open, oil leaked, the power steering was faulty, the paint jobs were poor. The car's odd vertical grill and overall looks got thumbs-down reviews from design mavens.

What else could be wrong? Ford's timing for the Edsel launch coincided with a shift in the U.S. auto market that was driven by a stiff recession that began in 1957. It was the dawn of the compact car era, with consumers rejecting so-called chromeliner sedans from Detroit that featured huge tail fins and low gas mileage in favor of more cost-efficient alternatives such as the Volkswagen Beetle.

The Edsel went on its way down the boulevard of broken dreams toward an ultimate destination in the lexicon of failure, costing Ford an estimated $350 million for its trouble.

3

PAPER PROFITS

Fashion is a little like the weather in Chicago. If you don't like it, just wait for twenty minutes and it will change. Some people see this characteristic of the garment industry as admirably dynamic, others are less charitable in their descriptions.

In the 1960s, some sixty clothing manufacturers thought they had hit it big with an innovation in materials use that took the idea of disposables to new heights, or depths, depending on your point of view. The hot new craze was paper clothing, and the idea for it didn't come out of a designer showroom. It came from a very conservative paper company in Philadelphia that was really interested in selling paper towels, napkins, and toilet paper.

The Scott Paper Company triggered an international mania for paper clothes when it offered paper dresses by mail to buyers of its "Color Explosion" line of household paper products. For only $1.25, "every girl can have a paper dress to call her own," read Scott's promotional literature. The Scott dresses were called "Paper Capers," and they were made from a specially treated paper that was fire resistant. The style was sleeveless paper bag all the way and only two prints, paisley and op art, were offered.

Within six months, Scott had sold more than half a million of the dresses, and the success of the promotion took the fashion world by storm. Here was the ticket to incredible sales growth—cheap disposable clothes.

The market, and throwaway choices, mushroomed. There were paper wedding gowns and maternity dresses. There were paper bikinis and paper resort wardrobes. You traveled without luggage, bought your clothes at the vacation site, and threw them away when you went home. The rich and famous—the Duchess of Windsor, Princess Lee Radziwill, the Beatles—all wore garments fashioned from paper. A charity ball in Connecticut sent invitations asking women attending to come dressed in paper.

It was as if the fashion industry had discovered the Holy Grail. Marketers saw logarithmic sales growth. The press predicted permanence for the era of disposables, with *Time* magazine noting that paper clothing was apparently "here to stay."

It wasn't. Paper clothing turned out to be a fast fading fad. Designers didn't really like paper. It was hard to work with, and after all, it just doesn't last. This was enough to cut paper clothes out of the market and shred the profit dreams of those who doted on disposables.

A PANNED PIZZA

People like pizza in a pan, and this preference has made thick-crusted pizza a profit center in many successful Italian restaurants. So you couldn't blame the decision by Godfather's pizza chain to add the item to its menus in 1984. Pan pizza was a winner with what seemed to be a minimum of risk. And Godfather's needed a winner to boost lagging earnings.

The restaurant company spent lots of money developing its entry into the pan pizza derby. It came up with a complicated recipe that took Godfather's employees lots of time to prepare. There were reports of workers beginning to make dough balls for crust at four in the morning, long hours before the arrival of any customers.

This pushed up labor costs and, with high ingredient costs added to the mix, Godfather's had a very expensive pan pizza to offer hungry eaters.

Maybe it was the price. Maybe it was the taste. Probably it was both. The new pizza wasn't popular, and Godfather's yanked it from the menu.

A cheaper version was eventually reintroduced, but the restaurant chain's deep desire for easy profits in deep-dish pizza was burned.

5

Not the Real Thing

There are few companies in the world with the marketing savvy and clout of the Coca-Cola Company. But even the great ones stub their toes every now and again, and when the mighty fall, their tumbles are resounding.

From the moment its executives unveiled the drink called New Coke in the spring of 1985, Coca-Cola knew it had a big problem on its hands. The new product was intended to replace the beverage Coca-Cola drinkers had been quaffing faithfully for a century.

There had been some changes in the formula for Coke since a pharmacist John Styth Pemberton created it. For example, corn syrup replaced cane sugar, but despite the change in sweeteners, company executives insisted that the soft drink's taste not be altered. The New Coke was supposed to boldly go where it had never gone before, into a new realm of taste that would put it back ahead of arch rival Pepsi.

Since 1972, Pepsi's taste-based challenge to Coke had been picking up momentum. Commercials featuring blind taste tests by consumers showed Pepsi consistently winning. And it wasn't just Madison Avenue hype. Coca-Cola's own private research was confirming the result, and Pepsi was also starting to outsell Coke in supermarkets.

If this trend became destiny, Coke might soon be the number two cola—an unacceptable possibility to the people in charge.

The decision was taken to do what until then had been the unthinkable—change the drink's taste to win the Pepsi challenge. After much time in the lab, researchers finally developed a new formula that was consistently favored in taste tests, not only over Pepsi, but also over the old Coke. The New Coke was born, sweeter than the original, to take on the pretender from PepsiCo in the battle for the taste buds of cola fanciers.

Somehow, what worked in the lab waffled in the marketplace. Coke execs knew that the shift carried some risk with it among the old Coke's faithful, but they had no idea the negative reaction to the replacement would be as powerful as it almost instantly became. Loyal Coke drinkers flooded the company's Atlanta headquarters with complaints. Callers compared New Coke to sewer water, furniture polish, and maybe worst of all, two-day-old Pepsi. People hoarded the old Coke against the feared day when it would no longer be on grocers' shelves. One wine store in Beverly Hills collected five hundred cases of the endangered drink and sold each one for $30, triple the normal price. An organization named the Old Coke Drinkers of America found willing participants for rallies and direct-mail campaigns to right the grievous wrong. There was even talk of a class-action suit to stop the alleged "progress."

The outcry worked. Less than ninety days after introducing the new product, Coca-Cola announced it would bring back the original formula drink and market it under the name Classic Coke.

The rest, as they say, is marketing history. There is no more New Coke, and there hasn't been for years. The original Coke is as strong as ever, having beaten back the Pepsi challenge with its market superiority intact. It's all worked out so well for Coke that some have suggested the whole New Coke gambit was a brilliant ploy to reinvigorate customer loyalty.

Neither ploy nor brilliant, the New Coke was just what it appeared to be—a magnificent miscalculation that unintentionally added up to success.

A "Healthy" Smoke?

6

THE SEARCH FOR HEALTHY CIGARETTES

You have to hand it to tobacco executives. Their attempts to shield consumers from the actual health consequences of smoking have taken some quite elegant forms. Among these, the history of Real cigarettes ranks high on the list.

Real was developed by R. J. Reynolds in an attempt to ride the crest of the "all-natural" product craze of the late 1970s. It was billed as a cigarette with nothing artificial added, and the tobacco company's executives were so confident of the new brand's success that they eschewed test marketing in favor of a direct move to national distribution. There was agreement that Real couldn't miss as the most successful brand introduction in the recent history of the cigarette business.

But, Real did miss, by a lot. Reynolds had overestimated the "health" motivation of smokers, although it was difficult to understand how that had happened, since people who smoke are knowingly introducing carcinogens into their bodies and, by definition, have to rank low on any scale of health motivation. Not surprisingly, hoped-for sales to the health-conscious consumers failed to materialize. You can't help but wonder what RJR had been smoking when thinking that health-conscious people would welcome a new cigarette.

And, of course, none of this involves the marketing oxymoron involved in promoting Real as a "healthier" cigarette.

After spending $40 million on advertising and free samples, RJR got real and pulled the all-natural smoke from the shelves in 1980. But the company's search for something "healthy" to smoke was hardly over. It was a search that brought the media to an elaborate press conference in New York's Grand Central Station in 1987. The event was the unveiling of the smokeless cigarette, Premier, which was touted as the world's "cleanest cigarette."

Premier gave smokers a kick without actually burning. Its design used a carbon element at the front which the smoker held a match to and then pulled air through. The heated air passed over a pinch of tobacco and something called "flavor beads," held in an aluminum capsule right behind the carbon tip.

The by-now-nicotine-imbued-smoky-tasting hot air in the Premier next passed through a filter before its trip to the smoker's lungs. And this was supposed to be the revolutionary product to unseat Marlboro?

True, Premier was smokeless, and that was okay. But the list of pluses stopped there. From start to finish, Premier had problems of the first magnitude. It was almost impossible to light, with some suggesting a blowtorch as a good ignition device. Drawing air through a Premier was so difficult that the term "hernia effect" was coined to describe the difficulty. And the payoff in taste and smell was compared with human solid and gaseous waste.

After four months on the market in 1988, Premier was retired with losses calculated at $325 million. Refusing to declare the experience a failure, RJR again went back to the smokeless cigarette drawing boards and by the mid-1990s was talking about an improved smokeless successor—something with the hopeful name Eclipse.

BELIEVE IT OR NOT, A BABY JESUS DOLL

You Don't Have to Be Jewish to Love Levy's went a famous advertising slogan for a New York bread baker. And, as it turns out, you don't have to be Christian to be moved by a trip to the Vatican.

Ben Mitchom, the Jewish president of the Ideal Toy Company, was so inspired by his 1957 visit to the Holy See that he decided to create a Baby Jesus doll. What Christian parent would not want his or her child to have a doll that honored Christianity's most-loved figure?

There were lots of doubters about the project, but then Christ had had his doubters too. The Most Wonderful Story doll made its debut in an elaborate package that looked like a large Bible. It came complete with a bed of straw and cardboard figures of the Holy Family.

Ideal had a strong position in the children's doll market, but not even the company's track record, or its marketing muscle, could move the doll off toy store shelves. They simply didn't sell, and you might guess the reasons why, which in his post-Vatican glow, Ben Mitchom failed to consider.

Anyone with young children knows the rough treatment they give their toys. Parents did not relish the thought of Baby Jesus being dragged upstairs by the hair or left lying in the middle of the living room.

Toy store owners and salespeople had similar concerns about Baby Jesus receiving the respect he deserved. They hoped the doll would sell, but were reluctant to create price inducements to move the merchandise. "How can you mark down Jesus Christ?" was the difficult question.

The ending to what has been called one of the biggest mistakes in the history of toys was anything but wonderful for the Ideal Toy Company. It was forced to buy back all the unsold inventory of Most Wonderful Story dolls.

THE OOBIE CLAMS UP

Oops on the Oobie

The Oobie was a plastic clam-shaped toy with two eyes and an address label on it. Developed by Parker Brothers in the early 1970s, the Oobie was supposed to be an ambassador of friendship sent from child to child.

The idea was for a child to write a note to a friend, put it in an Oobie, and write the friend's address on the outside. Parker Brothers' idealistic notion was that a child could leave an Oobie anywhere, and whoever happened to come upon the little clam would stop, pick it up, and help it along its journey across the street or across the country.

Not surprisingly, parents took a dim view of this reliance on the potential kindness of strangers. After all, a pervert might find the Oobie as easily as a child or more purely motivated adult, with the address on the toy providing a handy reason for an unwanted surprise visit.

End of story. End of the Oobie.

Not a Pretty Picture(phone)

It is one of the most touching scenes in Stanley Kubrick's classic science fiction film, *2001*. A moonbound scientist calls his young daughter from outer space on a telephone that allows them to see each other's picture and hear each other's voice, thanks to the wonders of modern technology provided by AT&T.

Back in the late 1960s, when *2001* was playing in theaters, it seemed a good bet that by the year 2001 the picturephone would be the kind of everyday communications device that Kubrick envisioned. While there's still some time for this scenario to become a reality before the beginning of the next millennium, it's a long shot that most of us will be seeing and hearing each other over the telephone by then.

AT&T's attempts to commercialize the picturephone are a daunting lesson in the difficulty of turning great leaps ahead in technology into profitable products.

Shortly after debuting the "see-as-you-talk phone" at the 1964 New York World's Fair, Ma Bell made the revolutionary service available in New York, Chicago, and Washington, D.C. There were high hopes for the innovation, despite the fact that a picturephone call cost twenty times an ordinary call, arrangements to use the new technology had to be made in advance by regular phone, and customers had to go to a special location to actually have the conversation.

The novelty never caught on, but AT&T remained undaunted. By 1970, it had an improved version of the picturephone technology ready for what it anticipated would be heightened consumer demand. There were projections of the sale or lease of a hundred thousand phones in five years, with the prediction that phones with pictures would be "widely used by the general public" by the 1980s.

Again, the marketplace put the picturephone on hold.

By 1992, AT&T was back, this time with a device named VideoPhone 2500. Less cumbersome than earlier generations, and equipped with a flip-up two- by two-and-a-half-inch color screen, this version of the "breakthrough" system was faster than older models, but its picture quality was much inferior to the full motion video and synchronized audio of television. People looked like they were forever caught in a badly dubbed movie.

Despite these failures, technology continues to move ahead, with the promise of the information highway making telephones that provide the visual and aural experience of television something that future generations of communicators may find commonplace. But when the history of telecommunications is written, there will be a long chapter reserved for the hyping of picturephones long before their economics and performance made them truly viable as a consumer product.

THE ELEVEN-MILLION-GALLON MISUNDERSTANDING

The night was clear, and the moon was yellow. And the oil came spilling out. So it went the night of Good Friday, March 24, 1989, in Alaska's Prince William Sound. The *Exxon Valdez*, an oil tanker the length of the Empire State Building, ran onto the rocks and into the headlines after leaving the port of Valdez. In the worst oil spill in American history, the crippled ship would eventually dump some eleven million gallons of thick crude oil into one of the world's most pristine marine environments.

The accident caused special outrage when it was discovered that the tanker's captain, Joseph Hazelwood, had been seen drinking before boarding ship the night of the accident, and that he had a long-term drinking problem Exxon knew about.

But the strongest public rage was triggered by television news pictures of the aftermath of the disaster. Reports of Exxon's first attempts to clean up the spilled oil showed workers using *rags* to wipe off rocks coated with the dark brown goo that was washing up, ankle deep, on hundreds of miles of island and coastal beaches. It was a task that made the work of Sisyphus, the mythological Corinthian king condemned forever to again and again push a heavy rock up a high hill, seem easy by comparison. Other news pictures showed oil-soaked birds, sea otters, and other wildlife. Some were dead, others were dying. Each image was more damning than the next. After all, this was no distant oil spill off the coast of France or the Middle East. This was the last American frontier and the touchstone of every urban dweller's untouched nature fantasy that was being slimed with the killer crude.

You might think that Exxon, one of the world's largest companies, would have instantly put all its public relations muscle behind an effort to tell its side of the spill cleanup story, with such an effort led by the company's chief executive. There were plenty of templates to follow, especially the reaction of Johnson & Johnson in the early 1980s when some of its Tylenol product was poisoned. A fast and official mea culpa from the CEO, uttered at the site of the crime, was the medicine many public relations pros suggested was Exxon's only hope for even modest control of the damage to the company's image.

In Valdez, Alaska, for the first two weeks after the spill, Exxon public relations and operations executives did hold extended press conferences twice a day, but no matter how cooperative they might have been, there was no voice from the top to lend urgency to the situation.

It wasn't until April 18, more than three weeks after the accident, that Exxon Chairman Lawrence G. Rawls visited Valdez and the spill area. He didn't go sooner, Rawls said, because there was nothing he could do to help the cleanup effort. Somehow, Rawls failed to understand that demonstrating his human concern about the disaster with an immediate visit to the site was as important to the public as anything Exxon might be doing to pick up the spilled oil.

In fact, the Exxon cleanup effort was the most massive operation of its kind ever mounted, lasting years and costing more than $2 billion. It *was* slow to get started, mostly because the equipment necessary to mount the cleanup had to be shipped to Alaska from distant locations. This took time. Meanwhile, the media took pictures of people wiping rocks with rags.

Postmortems of the *Exxon Valdez* disaster often mention arrogance, ignorance, stupidity, and bureaucratic rigor mortis as some of the reasons that the giant oil company was unable to handle its PR problems in a way that might have made public opinion more sympathetic.

Was it the public relations botch of all time? If not, it was close, and certainly memorable as a textbook case of how *not* to manage a corporate crisis.

CRYSTAL PEPSI:
A CLEAR LOSER

The television commercial was promoting a new product named Crystal Gravy, the sauce that allows you to "see your meat." It was a spoof, courtesy of the network television comedy show *Saturday Night Live*, but the message was telling. There was something about most clear products—especially foods—that didn't quite work.

Remember Clear Tab, a see-through soft drink, or Miller Clear, a transparent beer? Don't worry if you don't. Their passage was so brief as to be almost unnoticeable.

Of all the clear mistakes consumer product companies made in the late 1980s and early 1990s, possibly Crystal Pepsi was the biggest, if only because it received the most hype. The drink was introduced in early 1992, and just did not perform, generating less than half the sales Pepsi expected.

There is an old adage that goes "Fool me once, shame on you. Fool me twice, shame on me." You might think that PepsiCo's initial experience with Crystal Pepsi ("Fool me once") would have been enough and that the company would have pulled the product and written off its mistake. That's what other companies with clear disasters did. But PepsiCo persisted, reformulating, repackaging, and reintroducing Crystal Pepsi in 1994 ("Fool me twice"). Again, the results were unimpressive.

By that time, marketing pros were eulogizing the clear product fad, noting that consumers weren't anxious to pay higher prices for clear products that seemed to have fewer ingredients. They added that clear drinks such as colas were especially off base because they violated a consumer's long-standing expectations about such a drink's color.

A clear cola, they noted, had about as much taste appeal as brown water.

HUFFY'S WRONG
PEDAL PUSHERS

The concept at the $700 million Huffy bike company was fascinating—to combine all that was best in a mountain bike and a racing bike in a new product that would appeal to a racer's wish for speed and a climber's need for durability. When Huffy asked people in shopping malls about it, they said it sounded great. And when Huffy built it, it had high hopes that the new bike would be a winner. So what gave the Huffy Cross Sport bicycle a flat tire when it hit the market in the summer of 1991?

The high-tech hybrid carried a stiff-for-Huffy price tag of $159, some 15 percent more than the company's other models. To soften the sticker shock, some careful explanation of the new bike's superiority demanded some special selling at the retail level.

The kind of crack salespeople Huffy needed to explain the Cross Sport's value mostly work in specialty bike shops. Unfortunately, Huffy shipped the lion's share of its Cross Sport production to mass market retailers such as Kmart and Toys "R" Us, where the sales staff may be courteous and attentive, but not always well versed on the subtleties of product strengths.

So the glories of the Huffy Cross Sport stayed largely a secret, as bike buyers opted for less costly models. Huffy CEO Richard L. Molen called the bungled marketing plan a $5 million mistake, and within a year Cross Sport production had been cut 75 percent.

A Decision from Mars on E.T.

To make its extraterrestrial just that little bit more lovable, the producers of the megahit movie *E.T.* came to the M&M division of the Mars Candy Company in New Jersey to find a candy that their out-of-this-world star could munch.

M&M, fearing that its image might be sullied by the association with an alien life form, even if it did prefer candy that melted in its mouth and not in its elongated fingers, said no to the *E.T.* tie-in.

Next stop, H. B. Reese Candy Co., whose chocolate and peanut butter Reese's Pieces became the candy preference of E.T., and the millions of children who wound up loving him.

A Fruitless, Freeze-Dried Flop

14

JUST ADD MILK

America's push to put men on the moon in the 1960s was among the most extraordinary technological accomplishments of all time. It involved great leaps forward in rocketry, information processing, materials science, communications, and other fields.

Among the innovations, NASA developed a process of flash freezing foods and placing them in a high-pressure vacuum to remove all the moisture. With this freeze-dried nourishment on board, America's astronauts needed only to add water to create an acceptable meal of instant food and drink so far from the comforts of home.

In 1964, Post found a way to use the space technology to make the first meal of the day more fun. With freeze drying it was now possible to package a cereal with fruit already in the box. An experiment with freeze-dried strawberries added to corn flakes was a surprise hit. Next came cereals with freeze-dried blueberries and peaches with corn flakes, and Post made plans to build a factory for the exclusive production of its space-inspired new line of breakfast treats.

Not to be outdone, Kellogg quickly set out to better the competition with its own freeze-dried specialty, Corn Flakes with Instant Bananas. Promotions were to have featured the suitably corny Jimmy Durante promoting the new product by singing the lyric "Yes, we now have bananas" to the melody of the old familiar tune "Yes, We Have No Bananas."

The would-be promotion turned out to be an accurate premonition. We have no bananas, or other freeze-dried fruits, in cereals today because of a little timing problem that occurs when you add milk to the mix of cereal flakes and fruit chips that have been freeze-dried. It took some ten minutes of soaking for the fruit to reconstitute, and after ten minutes of soaking, not many people were interested in eating the soggy mass of mush, once crisp corn flakes, that was left in the cereal bowl.

After sampling the first boxes of cereal with freeze-dried fruit inside, few consumers became return customers, and the potential high-flying new breakfast spin-offs of the space program were grounded.

15

The Demise
of "the Beer That
Made Milwaukee Famous"

Without the Civil War, Milwaukee might never have had a heyday as the beer capital of America. The war brought a $1.00 tax on a gallon of whiskey, which was the drink of choice in the city's saloons. It also brought a $1.00 tax on a barrel of beer. Since there were thirty-one gallons in a beer barrel, a strong incentive for beer consumption was created in Milwaukee taverns, where the price of a tax-adjusted glass of whiskey suddenly became prohibitive to a citizenry with a fondness for penny-pinching.

In the decades that followed, the growth of national brands brewed in Milwaukee—Blatz, Miller, Pabst, Schlitz—was a source of civic pride, not to mention employment. By 1947, Schlitz had become the world's leading beer producer. Its advertising proudly proclaimed it "the Beer That Made Milwaukee Famous," a somewhat delusional claim. Whatever else Milwaukee might have been, it was certainly anything but famous. As recently as the 1970s Schlitz was the second-leading brand in America.

Schlitz beer was the centerpiece of lots of good times in Milwaukee, especially in the years after World War II. The company sponsored block parties, fireworks displays, and circus parades. Today, after more than a century of success, Schlitz beer is mostly a memory in Milwaukee and elsewhere. Its brewery, a magnet for tourists, school field trips, and other visitors, has housed an insurance company and other service businesses for years. The Schlitz brand is still brewed and distributed by the Stroh Brewery Company of Detroit, which bought the one-time pride of Milwaukee in 1981 and shortly after moved it out of town. But don't look for Schlitz on lists of best-selling brews. It hasn't been there for years.

What happened to the self-proclaimed Milwaukee fame maker is an excellent example of the old adage: "If it ain't broke, don't fix it," and a warning to executives with ideas about changing successful products. It's not unusual for brands to lose out in the marketplace due to changing consumer tastes, competition, and related factors. In the case of Schlitz, it almost looked as if the company set out to ruin a proud franchise.

There were key changes in the beer's ingredients and brewing process. Corn syrup was substituted for barley and fermentation time was cut by 300 percent. The result was a less expensive product that simply didn't taste as good as the original Schlitz. The final indignity was the addition of new foam-stabilizing chemicals that reportedly reacted with the beer to form tiny flakes. In 1976, some ten million cans of "the Beer That Made Milwaukee Famous" were recalled and destroyed, a debacle from which the company was never able to recover.

Within five years, Schlitz had been sold, shuttered, and moved out of Milwaukee. The demise of Schlitz, recalled a former mayor, was like the sinking of the *Titanic:* "How could that big business go under so fast?"

A New Flame

16

THE UNWAXED CANDLE
THAT WANED

In the late 1960s, Ronson, the company that was already famous for its flick-open lighter, was looking for a way to build sales of butane lighter fluid. The problem with cigarette lighters, it decided, was that people used them for only a few seconds at a time. Even the heaviest smokers were good for only a couple of minutes of lighter burn each day.

The solution was to enter the candle market with a new product that would beat wax models in longevity. And hope burned brightly in Ronson executive suites when the brushed aluminum Veraflame Butane Candle went to market. The reckoning was that an ultra-long-burning candle with a high-tech flair would be a hot item among gift buyers. An adjustable flame was a key selling feature, with Ronson ads touting low flames for intimate dinners, medium illumination for dinner parties, and high heat for swinging soirées. How could an antiquated candle compete with something that you could adjust to your moods and almost never burned out?

Quite easily, as it turned out. The insurmountable problem with the Ronson metal candle turned out to be what it cost. A price tag of $30 was too much to keep Veraflames burning in the marketplace.

17

What Was Killing Fields?

W. C. Fields is famous for letting the world know that, when all was said and done, he'd rather be in Philadelphia. Maybe that was because he had been bedeviled by a recurring nightmare of being stranded in a foreign city with no money.

As a hedge against the unhappy dream coming true, Fields opened some seven hundred bank accounts around the world. His deposits ranged from a few dollars to $50,000. And Fields used some highly creative pseudonyms on his accounts: Figley E. Whitesides, Colmonley Frampton-Blythe, and Elmer Mergetroid-Haines were a few.

The portly comedian turned out to be better at making up those names than in remembering where he kept his accounts. Able to recall only twenty-three places where he had money stashed when he died, Fields is estimated to have lost $1.3 million he just forgot about.

BAD FIT

18

Du Pont's Corfam: Better Losing Through Chemistry

When Du Pont unveiled it in the mid-1960s, the company hailed Corfam—a leather substitute—as the most important synthetic product since nylon and Dacron. The hardy material, a combination of polyester and polyurethane, had been thoroughly tested and seemed perfectly suited to take over the shoe industry. Corfam wore like iron, retained its shape, repelled water yet was porous. How could it miss?

Within months of its introduction, Corfam had the look of a major winner for the chemical giant. More than thirty shoe manufacturers were using it in more than a hundred different styles of shoes. The results emboldened the usually conservative Du Pont to project that by the mid-1980s, one out of every four American feet would be covered with Corfam.

With other manufacturers readying plans for everything from Corfam briefcases to basketballs, it seemed that the new material's success was guaranteed. Du Pont's stock shot to record prices, fueled by the enthusiasm about Corfam.

By 1971, Americans had reportedly bought a hundred million pairs of Corfam shoes, but Du Pont wasn't rolling in profits from Corfam's market penetration. In fact, the company had been losing a dollar on each pair of synthetic shoes that were being sold. The root of the problem was Corfam's cost. Du Pont had to sell it at a loss to sell it at all. Worse, consumers over time found Corfam shoes to be uncomfortable. They got too hot and never seemed to break in properly. Comfy old leather was hard to beat.

To the probable chagrin of millions of cows, but unlamented by humans, Du Pont finally pulled the plug on Corfam in the early 1990s. But ending production couldn't erase the material's legacy as a loser, a memory destined to be as indestructible as Corfam itself.

19

No Joy
at La Choy

La Choy is a well-known brand in grocery products, a name that shoppers trust for quality in middle-of-the-road prepared Chinese cuisine. Seeking to capitalize on growing consumer demand for low-fat foods, La Choy introduced its Fresh and Lite line of frozen entrees in 1988.

From the start, there were problems, and they began with the name. Marketing experts noted that Fresh and Lite was not the most appetizing appellation, sounding more like a feminine hygiene product than something you would want to eat. Next came the problem that Fresh and Lite was frozen food, not really fresh in the truest sense of the world.

But the biggest problem of all might have been with the Fresh and Lite egg rolls. Designed to be hearty enough for a whole meal, they took more than half an hour to cook in an oven—much longer than the time for delivery of a truly fresh-cooked meal from a Chinese restaurant. And if you popped one of the egg rolls into your microwave straight from the freezer, you tended to get a relatively unappetizing soggy log for your trouble.

With difficulties like these, Fresh and Lite turned out to be a heavy drag on La Choy profits, and the line was jettisoned within two years of its launch.

20

No Cadillac
of an Import Killer

When the complete history of the end of the twenti-eth century is written, it will be remembered, among other things, as the age of the yuppie in America. These young, affluent, well-educated urban professionals who were born after World War II raised conspicuous consumption to a high art and a level unseen before in the U.S.

Among the most-desired yuppie trophies of the period, the right imported luxury car was high on the list. European BMWs and Mercedeses were the vehicles of choice, with the Lexus or Infiniti from Japan an acceptable, if not quite so desirable, alternative.

In an attempt to win sales in this important market segment, the Cadillac division of General Motors went to the drawing boards to design a sporty import-killing car that any yuppie could love. The result was the Allanté, which debuted in 1987 with the shocking sticker price of $54,000.

It almost seemed that the design principle of "less is more" was used to create the car. The Allanté looked pretty enough, but it was less powerful, less quiet, less roomy, less leak-proof, and more expensive than much larger traditional Cadillacs.

No one suggested it, but you couldn't be blamed if you thought that the Allanté somehow embodied Cadillac's contempt for its target market's intelligence. Not surprisingly, the car sat in dealer showrooms, even after GM came out with a new version that featured a much more powerful engine and other engineering upgrades.

It was too little, too late. The Allanté, the wannabe import killer from Cadillac, died a quick death in the marketplace.

21

A Rose by
Any Other Name . . .

Bernard Baruch said he got rich by selling too soon. The same could not be said of Lana Turner's grandfather. He was one of the first major investors in the Coca-Cola soft drink company. He thought the drink tasted all right, but he was sure Coke would flop using what he thought was a horrible name.

So he sold out fast and invested in another cola company whose name he liked a lot more. Remember the Raspberry Cola Corporation?

SINGULAR FLOP

GERBER'S BOTTLED BABY BUNGLE . . .

Among the icons of American marketing, probably none is as enduring, heartwarming, or alluring as the Gerber baby. How could any mother resist the wide-eyed, openmouthed beckoning of this cherub on the label when perusing the alternatives among bottled purées of peas and carrots, plums and pears, chicken and beef on grocers' shelves?

There are some who might suggest the Gerber baby is almost too cute for comfort, but that wasn't the problem Gerber encountered with its potent selling symbol when it began marketing its baby foods in Africa.

In many African countries, what you see on the label is what you get in the bottle. Somehow, Gerber was unaware of this tradition, and used its famous baby picture labels on bottles and cans of baby food destined for the tummies of Africa's babies.

Needless to say, not much made it there.

. . . AND ITS SLIPUP WITH SINGLES

In the 1970s, Gerber thought that its brand could be extended to adults too. After all, most of America grew up on Gerber baby foods, so why should the company have to give up those customers just because they grew teeth and outgrew their diapers?

The company studied the demographics of the nation and chose single people living alone as its best hope for high sales. To win them, Gerber concocted a meal-for-one-in-a-jar line of products that it sold in baby food–style jars.

Named Singles, the line included lots to choose from that bore no resemblance to the mashed peas or bananas that were such staples with the toddler crowd. Gerber's grown-up delights included international offerings such as beef burgundy, Mediterranean vegetables, and sweet-and-sour pork.

But despite the company's attempt to distance its

adult fare from baby stuff, the Singles market wasn't able to make the emotional leap. Adults couldn't get past the baby food image, and the new product's name—Singles—also reminded them of what was all too often the pain of their solitary status.

For Gerber, Singles turned out to be a singular failure.

24

THE SAD SAGA
OF SUZY

The private sector has no exclusive on I.Q.–challenged business decisions. Governments do lots of forehead-slapping things too. Consider the case of the Susan B. Anthony dollar, named for the nineteenth-century suffragette and mother of the twentieth-century constitutional amendment giving women the right to vote.

When it was introduced in July 1979, the commemorative coin was supposed to be a government economy measure, saving an estimated $50 million a year in the printing costs of paper money and $100 million in building a new paper money printing plant.

The Suzy, as the currency was dubbed, had lots of alleged practical advantages too. It fit into vending machines and was easily identifiable by the visually handicapped because it had eleven sides. The first U.S. currency to carry the image of a woman other than the

Statue of Liberty, the bright and shiny Susan B. Anthony dollar would also save people the embarrassment of having to use dirty dollar bills, said U.S. Mint officials.

The logic of a dollar coin was compelling. Coins can be used for thirty years, while paper money needs to be replaced in about eighteen months. The problem was, however, that people just don't seem to want a dollar coin. A metal Eisenhower dollar had flopped just years before the Suzy was introduced, and market research continued to show people against a metal dollar by a ratio of five to one.

Understanding all this (but apparently understanding very little) the Treasury ordered production of 840 million Susan B. Anthony dollars anyway.

Predictably, the public rejected the coin in a hurry. It clogged up everyone's pockets. It felt more like a quarter and people had trouble telling the difference. Probably worst of all, the new dollar's dimensional similarity to the twenty-five-cent coin made everyone feel poorer—a reminder of how inflation had literally been shrinking the value of their money.

Some 525 million of the shiny Susan B. Anthony dollars never made it out of the Treasury Department's vaults, and the hoped for reduction in paper money production costs never materialized.

25

What Spoiled
Campbell's Fresh Thinking

With visions of new market niches dancing in their heads, Campbell Soup executives went on a new product spree in the 1980s, releasing an average of some 160 new products a year.

One of the more interesting innovations was Campbell's Fresh Chef line of soups and salads. The hope for Fresh Chef was that it would become popular with consumers who had had enough of frozen, prepackaged, ready-to-eat meals.

The theory was appealing, but the risks of inept execution were high. Fresh Chef was fresh, all right. It had a shelf life of only a week. If Campbell missed the mark on what meals would sell, there would be lots of spoilage, lots of disappointed customers, and lots of losses.

And that's exactly what happened as one mistake after another spoiled Campbell's fresh product push.

After racking up $25 million in losses, Campbell called it quits on Fresh Chef with this startling admission from one executive: "We never knew what to make."

No Sweet Smell of Success

26

THE WASHOUT OF
EAU DE BIC

Millions of Americans flick their Bics every day, and the Bic Corporation has made handsome profits selling its disposable cigarette lighters, pens, and razors.

Looking for a way to broaden its product offerings, Bic executives decided to get into the perfume business. While the logic of it all might seem a stretch, wasn't Bic already selling quite successfully one plastic-encased liquid that people used a little bit at a time? Why not another?

Bic went into the perfume business at the end of the 1980s with a product named Parfum Bic. It was an odd mix of American kitch and European continent that left observers scratching their heads over what Bic might have been thinking. The perfume's packaging, some said, looked suspiciously like a cigarette lighter and just wasn't at all feminine.

This was the wrong stuff on which to build sales of a new fragrance. Parfum Bic began turning in some malodorous financial results and in 1990 Bic flicked its perfume business into oblivion.

27

Dry Pie
in the Sky

Beer is made from lots of ingredients, but take away the malt, hops, yeast, and other stuff and what you have left is mostly water. And water is wet.

When we get thirsty, we go looking for wet things to drink. For centuries, beer has been one of the drinks humans have used to quench their thirsts. This is not only because beer is wet, but it's at least part of the reason.

So you have to wonder what the makers of some of the world's best-known beers were up to in 1990 when they spent upwards of $40 million on advertising to woo beer lovers into trying something new called *dry* beer. Anheuser-Busch, Coors, and a handful of foreign brewers all tried to put this oxymoronic offshoot at the top of best-selling beer lists.

Consumers not only had trouble tasting much that was different about dry beer (despite the name it was still wet), they also didn't have the patience to decode the claims of the new brew's abstract advantage— something beer executives said was a "cleaner finish."

Dry beer never appealed to more than 2 percent of America's beer drinkers, parching profit projections and leaving the ill-fated fluid's promoters second-guessing themselves. As one executive at Coors said: "Knowing what we do now, we probably wouldn't have gone with it."

28

THE MISDIRECTION AT VECTOR

You can't charge the Vector Automotive Corporation with limited ambition. The company is trying to create a super-upscale American sportscar on par with those powerful Italian status symbols, the Lamborghini and Ferrari.

And Vector is failing quite impressively.

In its first twenty years in the automobile business, Vector has managed to build only twenty-two cars while losing almost $30 million. You've heard of the gang that couldn't shoot straight. This is the car company that can't build right.

Tennis star Andre Agassi bought a Vector W8 in 1991. He paid $400,000 and almost immediately demanded a refund when he noticed a burning smell coming from the backseat during his first spin in the car. Hot exhaust pipes had almost ignited the car's carpeting, and Agassi's mechanic told him he was as good as riding in a time bomb on wheels.

Such problems appear to have been the rule rather than the exception for Vector. Especially unencouraging are the stories of battles between Gerry Wiegert, the company's founder, and managers who have had him ousted from the company because they saw Wiegert as one main reason for all the problems.

Among the charges: Wiegert's use of company funds to buy a bra for his wife. Wiegert shot back that it was a perfectly legitimate twenty-eight-dollar business expense because his wife needed the garment for an auto show.

Against the backdrop of this slapstick, the search for success at Vector continues, with the latest model under development pegged to sell at a bargain basement price of $189,000.

Will Vector make it with a car that won't threaten the lives and limbs of its owners this time? The company, realistic about its market position if nothing else, says it has nothing to lose and that its reputation has nowhere to go but up.

29

IBM's PCjr:
Out at Home

IBM is a legend in business. Its computers do large jobs, and small ones, for companies, governments, institutions—any organization that can use digital technology. But there is one market segment where IBM has not been dominant at all—home computer users.

The story of IBM's PCjr helps explain why.

IBM put the putative home PC on the market as "a bright little addition to the family." But the homey positioning didn't help initial sales, even when IBM cranked out a version of the machine that could play music.

The improvement didn't bring a happy sales tune with it either. No matter how it might be souped up, there was no way for the PCjr to be a winner. Its price tag was too high. Its microprocessor was too weak. Its keyboard was too cumbersome.

Despite a $40 million marketing push, the PCjr never caught on, making you wonder why IBM thought it could succeed with the machine in the first place.

STRANGE BREW

30

HOP'N GATOR BEER: HARD TO SWALLOW

Who hasn't seen the dousing of a National Football League coach with Gatorade spilling from an orange tub when his team wins a big game? Who doesn't know that basketball superstar Michael Jordan sips the stuff to help keep his performance at a peak?

Such media exposure has helped create the image of Gatorade as the winner's drink in the world of big-time sports. The beverage is the King of the Hill of sports drinks, the choice of certified jocks and aspiring athletes alike.

Gatorade comes in thirteen flavors and more than $1.2 billion of it was consumed in 1996. But it hasn't always been seashells and balloons for the sweetened electrolyte replacer. An attempt to mix Gatorade with beer in the search for expanded sales, for instance, went quickly down the drain.

The frankenbrew named Hop'n Gator beer came to

market in 1969. Mixing Gatorade, which rehydrates you, with beer, which dehydrates you, doesn't seem to make sense. But there are some who suggest that the rationale for putting the two together had to do with the way Gatorade speeds lost sodium and potassium into your system, a property of the drink that would work to speed the alcohol in beer into your system as well, increasing the kick.

"You may forget the name, but you'll never forget the taste," promised the ad slogan for Hop'n Gator.

As is the case with many ad slogans, it was somewhat wide of the truth. The taste was forgettable (as you might guess a mix of beer and gatorade would be) and the mix didn't sell.

31

KINKO'S:
COPIES OUTSIDE ITS RIGHTS

From a humble beginning with one copier in a converted California taco stand, Kinko's has grown into an international corporate colossus with more than eight hundred stores around the world offering advanced business services to the little guy.

Roughly one of four copies in the retail market for paper reproductions comes out of Kinko's copy machines. It's proven itself to be one smart outfit, but its corporate I.Q. didn't save it from a well-publicized blunder involving the no-no of copyright infringement.

Seemingly oblivious to the protection under copyright law given to the textbooks it was profitably copying and selling to students on college campuses, Kinko's got nailed by publishers in a copyright action that cost it a $1.9 million settlement in 1989.

Nowadays, Kinko's is still copying textbooks for kids on campus, but it gets the rights to do so first from the companies that publish the texts, and it pays appropriate royalties too.

ALL WET

32

SINKING

AMPHICAR SALES

"Why can't a woman be more like a man?" wonders Professor Henry Higgins in the play *My Fair Lady*.

We don't know if Hanns Trippel ever wondered why automobiles couldn't be more like boats, but we do know that he did design a car that could become a boat in the late 1950s. Trippel's Amphicar was billed as the perfect way for the coastal commuter to get to work: "Avoid Traffic and No Tolls."

In the water, the Amphicar's front wheels functioned as rudders, and two propellers to drive it were housed under the rear bumper. There were impressive-looking tailfins for styling panache.

Advocates also noted that Amphicar handled beautifully in heavy snow.

The double threat creation by Trippel, who had designed amphibious machines for the German war effort in World War II, also came with a price tag of $3,395.

The führer might have liked Trippel's designs, but the American market never really took to the water mobile, which was a terrible performance dud. Its four-cylinder engine could manage a top speed on land of only seventy-two miles per hour. In the water, the Amphicar was a slowpoke that couldn't do much better than five miles an hour.

Price was inversely related to performance. You could buy a regular car, boat, and trailer for less than you had to pay for the Amphibious slowpoke. But the most serious weakness of this admittedly charming idea might have been the unfortunate tendency of the Amphicar's bottom to rust out after having been in the water only a few times.

Within a few years, the Amphicar had sunk from the marketplace without a trace, although there are still a handful of enthusiasts who enjoy the little vehicle's unique pleasures.

33

GULP FICTION

William D. Smithburg loves to ski. So you have to wonder how the chairman and CEO of the Quaker Oats Co. failed to avoid the downhill run his company got from its 1994 acquisition of the Snapple Beverage Corp.

At the time of the Quaker buyout, Snapple was the darling of the so-called New Age flavored tea and fruit drink business. It was made out of the "Best Stuff on Earth," featured quirky ads with campy people, and seemed literally to fly off convenience store and grocery shelves.

Quaker bought Snapple with high hopes. So what if some wondered whether the $1.4 billion price tag for Snapple seemed a little high. This was an acquisition for the ages, went Quaker's rationale, with Snapple an excellent complement to Quaker's popular Gatorade line. This purchase was based on hard analysis, not wish fulfillment.

As it turned out, Snapple mixed with Quaker like,

well, iced tea and oatmeal. And in early 1997, less than three years after buying Snapple, Quaker sold it off for just $300 million, showing losses on the venture of almost $2 million a *day*.

The disaster began quickly and escalated. With bad timing that was hard to beat, Quaker bought Snapple at the peak of the New Age drink mania. Industry estimates show growth rates for flavored waters, juices, and teas like Snapple dropping from about 25 percent a year in 1994 to well under 10 percent annually in 1996. Heavy competition from soft drink giants Coke and Pepsi eroded Snapple's share of this slower-growing market, and the competition's more efficient production methods undercut Snapple on price.

In the New Age beverage wars, Snapple was getting crushed. Quaker attempted to fight back with new flavors and flashier packaging. The drinks had names like Mango Madness, Bali Blast, and Samoan Splash that seemed unconsciously to echo Snapple's embattlement and desperation, but the tropical terminology and even a giveaway program that reportedly cost $25 million in free drinks and other costs were hardly enough to turn around the embarrassment.

Quaker's dream of profits in New Age drinks had become a billion-dollar nightmare of red ink that Wall Street wags quickly labeled a case of "Gulp Fiction."

34

WHEN THE CHIPS ARE DOWN

The march of progress has been relentless at the Intel Corporation, the Santa Clara, California–based maker of computer chips. Ranked number sixty on *Fortune* magazine's list of America's 500 largest industrial companies in 1995, Intel jumped seventeen places to number forty-three at the end of 1996. Investors gave Intel the third-highest stock market valuation in 1996, up from fifth the year before on an astounding 11,000 percent increase in the price of Intel's stock multiplied by the company's number of shares outstanding.

Intel, it seems can do no wrong, so it makes the company's almost comically defensive handling of a bobble in 1994, when it was discovered that its Pentium chip had a calculation-affecting flaw, seem especially puzzling.

Intel's first response to the news of its fallibility was to maintain that there was really no problem. The company challenged Pentium users to come up with the evidence of flaws in the chips. When lots of examples of the problem flowed in, Intel's next step was to attempt to minimize the mess-up. Whatever the problem was, said Intel, it would affect only one calculation out of every nine billion. How serious could that be?

Serious enough to create a mistake in every few minutes of computer operation was the answer, and the customer protests continued. The issue came to a head when IBM stopped shipments of all computers with the Pentium inside, and said its analysis showed the potential for Pentium mistakes to be ninety times greater than Intel's estimate.

Eventually, Intel recalled the Pentiums at an estimated cost to the company of $500 million. Intel CEO Andrew Grove admitted the company had missed "the kernel of the issue," and that Intel had made a mistake in presuming "to tell somebody what they should or shouldn't worry about, or should or shouldn't do."

35

GENERALLY UNDYNAMIC

General Dynamics was a household name around the Pentagon in the 1950s and 1960s, selling warplanes, missiles, and other military hardware to keep the world safe for democracy.

But an idea from Howard Hughes set the military aircraft manufacturer in pursuit of profits in commercial airplane production, a field it had not previously explored. Hughes, the owner of TWA, wanted a plane for his airline from General Dynamics, and the company's top brass jumped at the idea.

With TWA as a major buyer, they foresaw sales of $1 billion, with profits of $250 million, in a decade. And there was lots of room for error. Even pessimistic projections of the venture showed profits of $50 million, and so the push to build the Convair 880 passenger plane was launched.

Despite the rosy vision from the executive suite, there

were doubters in the ranks who feared that the company would suffer from a venture into a field where it had no experience. Some worried that cost estimates were unreasonably low. Others questioned whether the company had the production capacity to fill orders without expanding. There was also the problem of Howard Hughes, whose reliability as a customer was unknown.

These fears became reality in what turned out to be, for the time, the record loser in a single commercial manufacturing project. General Dynamics ended up losing $425 million on the attempt to build a commercial carrier, almost one third of the company's net worth.

It seems incredible, but the cost of the new plane's parts was discovered to be more than the intended selling price of the plane itself. Estimates of the number of planes General Dynamics needed to sell to break even were much too low. Hoped-for orders from airlines other than TWA failed to materialize.

And when General Dynamics finally finished the first of the Convair line, Howard Hughes—by then the sole buyer of the aircraft—announced he couldn't pay.

The Convair 880 and a successor, the Convair 990, eventually did fly. But General Dynamics' dreams of profits on the airliners had long since vanished into thin air.

36

SNACKTIME SNAG

The search among toymakers to add lifelike characteristics to their creations is a time-honored practice.

The Cabbage Patch Snacktime doll was in that tradition. It was designed with a little motor and set of gears that powered the doll's jaw, allowing it to "eat" plastic carrots and cookies.

How cute.

But complaints about the doll to its maker, Mattel Corporation, might have harkened up visions of a scene in the 1960s sci-fi flick *Barbarella*, where Jane Fonda is munched on by the grinning sharp-toothed playthings of some sadistic little kids.

Shocked parents reported that the Snacktime doll's jaws had a fondness for children's hair and fingers as well as plastic food. The Consumer Product Safety Commission launched an investigation.

In response, Mattel announced a labeling program for

the doll, warning of its possible dangers and how to avoid them. And it began an internal probe of the dangers of the doll. Mattel wound up conceding it had not tested Snacktime for hair entanglement before sending it to market, but the company also pointed out the motor and gears it was using in the doll were standard toy industry issue.

Ultimately, Mattel took the doll off the market and offered buyers a full $40 refund. That decision cost it money, but won points with consumers which helped soften the Snacktime damage.

37

Coleco's Adam Computer:
The Genesis of Disaster

What's a nice toy company like you doing in the high-tech rat race of the computer business?

This paraphrase of the time-honored pickup bar question was logical to ask executives of Hartford, Connecticut–based Coleco Industries, Inc. when they sought to make a success of a home computer named Adam.

The $700 system was released in 1983 and almost immediately went south in the marketplace. After a big buildup and a carefully planned debut, the Adam turned out to be a major disappointment that was riddled with technical problems.

Coleco compounded its difficulties when it was unable to make enough Adams to meet demand for the all-important Christmas selling season. Product returns were also heavy, running far ahead of industry norms.

Persevering, Coleco improved the Adam, releasing a

new version with better technology and more software, but Adam's lousy image had already done the product in. One industry analyst noted it was going to be almost impossible "to resurrect a lemon like that" no matter how much Coleco might spend on advertising to burnish the Adam's image.

38

A FAMILY AFFAIR

When Pamela Digby Churchill Hayward Harriman died in 1997, the *Chicago Tribune* wrote, "In a grander era, she might have rivaled Louis XV's Madame de Pompadour as leading lady of a royal court, fabulous arts patron, charming salonist and one of the great social lionesses of history."

Before we continue, let us annotate her name. Born Pamela Digby in England in 1921, she first exchanged vows with Randolph Churchill, son of the British prime minister; next married Leland Hayward, producer of Broadway musicals including *South Pacific, Gypsy,* and *The Sound of Music;* and last espoused Averell Harriman, career politician, diplomat, and railroad fortune heir.

In addition to her three marriages, she is also reliably said to have had intimate dalliances with the likes of Edward R. Murrow, Prince Aly Khan, Jock Whitney, and numerous other men high on the list of the twentieth century's most rich and powerful.

But despite her various strengths, no one ever accused Pamela Harriman of being much of a money manager. Quite the contrary.

In late 1994, heirs to the Harriman trusts filed court papers alleging that a group of funds worth $25 million in 1989 had shrunk to less than $6 million in value. It seems that some very unprofitable real estate investments had been made in a marginal New Jersey resort that had begun life as part of Hugh Hefner's Playboy empire during its halcyon days.

Named in the lawsuit: Pamela Harriman, executor and a trustee of the Harriman fortune, and two distinguished Washington lawyers with long records of government service, Clark Clifford and Paul Warnke, whom Averell Harriman had hired to look after his estate. He had died in 1986, leaving an estimated $100 million to Pamela. After her death, the money was to go to Averell's children and grandchildren.

The crux of the dispute centered on a man named William Rich, who had actually made the bad investments. Clifford and Warnke were supposed to have been watching what Rich was doing, with Pamela following their advice on financial matters.

In their federal lawsuit, the Harriman heirs alleged that Pamela had urged the risky real estate investments, but Pamela denied all the charges. The public airing of this dirty blue-blooded laundry made the stuff of night-time television soap opera seem tame. A world-class courtesan charged with blowing the money of one of America's most distinguished families on the former pleasure palace of a soft-core pornographer? It seemed too delicious to be true.

The unseemly affair ended when an out-of-court settlement was reached among all warring parties. And as befits people with an impeccable background and breeding—an excellent description of all those involved in this messy family affair—the terms were undisclosed. But amid the charges and countercharges, there was never any doubt that some truly lousy investments had been made.

39

SIMPLESSELY DISAPPOINTING

T he search for a fat substitute that delivers all the taste and satisfaction of the real thing has been a quest of the food industry for years. To the winner of the race to produce something that could replicate the pleasure of eating fried chicken or ice cream without the consequences of consuming too much fat for good health will go the profits of unparalleled success.

When the federal Food and Drug Administration (FDA) gave a green light to Monsanto's Simplesse fat substitute in 1990, the company thought it might finally have made it to that long-sought finish line. The formula for Simplesse called for milk proteins and egg whites. The ingredients were then blended and heated. It was a natural product that the FDA okayed for use in frozen desserts. No need for safety studies here.

The first product containing Simplesse to reach consumers was Simple Pleasures, a frozen dessert that Monsanto was betting heavily on. But the early reviews were not quite what the company had hoped for.

While there were some enthusiastic first tasters, other reviewers complained of an unpleasant aftertaste, especially in Simple Pleasures' chocolate flavor. There seemed to be a consensus that, good as it might be, Simple Pleasures was probably not going to replace super-premium ice creams in the dessert dishes, hearts, and minds of Americans. Simplesse didn't lend itself to use in baking or frying, so its market potential was further limited.

Within a few short years, Simplesse was being talked about in the same breath with the Edsel and New Coke when all-time great product failure discussions took place. Although such a comparison might have been an exaggeration, even Monsanto executives admitted that their expectations for Simplesse were higher than they should have been.

40

THE GATES THAT
ROSS PEROT MISSED

Ross Perot is a highly successful billionaire with tons of ambition and charisma to match. Whether you love him or hate him, it's hard to ignore Ross Perot. But can you imagine where Perot might be today had he not missed his opportunity to buy out Bill Gates and take over Microsoft when the software giant was just getting started?

Perot took his shot at Microsoft in 1979. He was sure Gates was on the road to building a great company, but he wasn't sure how much to offer to buy Gates out.

There are different versions of how Perot's failed acquisition attempt actually went. Gates recalls asking Perot for between $6 million and $15 million for his company. Perot says Gates's asking price was more like $40 to $60 million. The numbers don't really matter much. From 1979, Microsoft went on a growth tear that has made it one of the world's most powerful compa-

nies. Bill Gates has become an entrepreneurial
and America's richest man.

Ross Perot knows he might have been that man, and
has admitted to regretting not paying up for Microsoft
when it was there for his taking. Perot considers his decision one of the biggest mistakes he has ever made.

Wrong, Ross. Considering Perot's convictions about
Microsoft's future, his confusion of price with value in
the blown buyout were strong. It's one of the biggest
business mistakes *anyone* has ever made.

TECHNOLOGICALLY ADVANCED TURKEY?

41

THE COLD RECEPTION FOR POLAVISION

Would you pay $675 for a camera that gave you a two-and-a-half-minute silent movie with a grainy picture?

Somehow, this was the proposition that executives at Polaroid thought consumers would rush to accept in the late 1970s when the company that popularized instant still photography came to market with the Polavision movie-in-a-minute system.

You have to wonder how Polaroid thought its Polavision could compete with the home video systems that were then becoming popular and gave users full-color, full-motion, and full-sound videotapes that ran for an hour and more. But somehow Dr. Edwin Land, the camera's creator, was convinced that Polavision would provide people with a new way to relate to life that would somehow translate into sales success.

His enthusiasm was not shared in the marketplace.

Polavision was scorned as being the "all-time turkey" in video systems. Store managers where the product was sold did not hesitate to call it a dud.

Curiously, Polariod seemed to think the problem with Polavision was on the consumer end, rationalizing that the system was too advanced technologically for the American public in the 1970s to fully grasp.

The U.S. Ski Team did use Polavision for a while to track downhill skiers, and there was some limited enthusiasm for Polavision as a teaching tool for golf and tennis instructors. Polaroid also tried to sell Polavision to doctors for use in the visual examination of internal organs.

But these niche marketing attempts were far from the mass market that Polaroid had envisioned and they didn't come close to putting Polavision in the black.

After two years and a $68 million loss, Polaroid hit the reject button on Polavision for good.

42

SelectaVision:
RCA's Bad Choice

Inside RCA it was called the "Manhattan Project," a conscious reuse of the code name given to the effort to produce America's first atomic bomb. The new product being developed in RCA's "Manhattan Project" was going to be just as explosive in the marketplace as a nuclear device, and work on it was shrouded in much the same secrecy that surrounded the A-bomb.

But despite the cloak-and-dagger approach, the result of this extraordinary new product development effort, RCA's SelectaVision videodisc, turned out to be a bomb that shattered the venerable consumer electronics producer's hopes for a breakthrough technology.

SelectaVision, a kind of video record player, was supposed to become a multibillion-dollar business for RCA. It was priced low for mass market appeal. It was as easy to use as a record player, and it promised the possibility of consumers building libraries of videodiscs of their favorite movies and television shows in the same way that they collected records. It seemed that RCA's billing of SelectaVision as "the most exciting new form of entertainment since television" was more than just promotional hype.

But that's what it turned out to be when SelectaVision was consigned to the scrap heap of new products that didn't quite make it after a few short years on store shelves.

Two basic problems torpedoed SelectaVision. Unlike VCRs, which were just coming into vogue when SelectaVision made its debut, the videodisc player could not record a program from a television broadcast or cable. This hurt, but by itself probably wasn't enough to doom the product. Most people didn't use VCRs as recording devices when SelectaVision came to market and still don't today.

But people do rent videotapes, and this turned out to be SelectaVision's Achilles' heel. When the product appeared, it had to compete with an established and growing video rental network for people to use with their VCRs. Tapes could be rented cheaply, and returned easily. There was no similar rental infrastructure to support videodisc players. RCA's belief that people would want

to own lots of videodiscs and build libraries turned out to be wrong. It was costly to buy a videodisc when you only wanted to watch a movie once or twice.

SelectaVision—RCA's great hope for a multibillion-dollar consumer electronics success—turned out to be a $580 million loss. The company had produced a technology that was okay, but its understanding of human nature was way off.

43

HE MISSED
HIS CALLING

If Chicago inventor Elisha Gray had played it a little differently, it's quite possible that he would have gone down in history as the inventor of the telephone instead Alexander Graham Bell.

Gray and Bell both invented telephones, but Gray's worked better. They filed for patent protection of their inventions almost simultaneously on Valentine's Day in 1876. Because of the dead heat, patent officials called for a ninety-day period of review to decide what to do.

During that time, Bell was more aggressive, and luck was on his side. While Gray stayed home, Bell went to Washington to make his case in person as the rightful inventor of the phone. Almost unbelievably, the patent examiner Bell met with was a big fan. The man was reportedly a deaf mute who had great admiration for Bell's work with the hearing impaired. In an extraordinary breach of protocol, he is said to have shown Gray's patent papers to Bell, apparently letting the cat out of the bag on how to build a better sound transmitter.

Into the margins of his patent documents, Bell wrote Gray's sound ideas, saying he had developed the same thing, but had forgotten to include it. And then he built the famous first phone on which he called, "Mr. Watson, come here, I want you," using Gray's sound transmitter.

Once he learned what had happened, Gray tried to recoup in court. He ultimately settled for cash and signed away all claims to the telephone.

What might have happened had Elisha Gray hotfooted it to Washington in the winter of 1876 to lobby for his invention? We'll never know. But for those of you who believe everything works out according to some grand design we can't perceive, it's hard to argue that a phone company that came to be known as "Ma Bell," and not "Ma Gray," wasn't somehow meant to be.

44

A Xerox Decision
That Didn't Compute

The machine had a mouse that clicked. Its screen showed you little pictures that let you do what you wanted when you clicked on them. It could be connected to other machines like itself. Its name was Alto and it was a personal computer, up and running in the Xerox corporation's Palo Alto, California, research center years before there were any similar machines from IBM, Apple, Compaq, Hewlett-Packard, or anyone else.

The personal computer was invented by Xerox, and was, in fact, used by lots of people in its California research facility in the 1970s. But it never made it out of the lab because of priority problems at company headquarters. Xerox management didn't want to spend the bucks necessary to commercialize the innovation, but the decision went deeper than just a money problem.

Xerox, which was the household name in document copying, couldn't think of itself as a computer company and so the Alto became what has been termed "the most important unannounced computer product of the 1970s."

Not surprisingly, many of the people who helped invent the PC for Xerox became frustrated and wound up playing important roles in developing the companies that did capitalize on making the desk-top digital machine almost as ubiquitous as the television and telephone.

45

FRIENDLY SKIES, UNFRIENDLY TESTS

When you get in an airplane in the United States for a domestic flight, your chances of dying in an accident are only about one in ten million. So there's no real argument that flying is dangerous, and the federal government, airlines, and airplane manufacturers have lots of rules and regulations designed to keep air travel safe. They are obviously doing an excellent job, but sometimes—despite the best intentions—things do happen that make you wonder about the I.Q.s of the people running these shows. Such a case took place in 1991.

To meet government safety requirements when an airplane's passenger capacity is increased, the McDonnell Douglas Corp. sought people to participate in evacuation testing of its reconfigured MD-11 aircraft. McDonnell Douglas was increasing the MD-11's capacity from about three hundred to four hundred passengers, a move that mandates tests to make sure everyone can get out of the plane within ninety seconds if something goes wrong.

In order to simulate actual emergency conditions, the federal regulations stipulated the use of people in the tests—not computer simulations, dummies, or some other methods. Most of the people ultimately involved in the tests were company employees, but some were recruited from a senior citizens center with the enticement of a $49 fee for participating. Older people were needed to meet Federal Aviation Administration (FAA) requirements for a cross section of passenger ages, and there weren't enough seniors on the McDonnell Douglas payroll to meet the quota.

The testing called for the human guinea pigs to walk through an obstacle-strewn darkened cabin to an emergency escape chute lowered from the plane. Next, they had to jump out and slide to the cement floor of an airplane hangar in near-total darkness. If everyone was out of the plane in a minute and a half, the federal government was satisfied, and McDonnell Douglas could sell the higher capacity model of the aircraft.

In the first round of tests, press reports cited 28 injuries in the evacuation of 421 people from the plane in 132 seconds. Some of those injured suffered broken bones. Despite the mishap, a second set of tests was run (McDonnell Douglas must *really* have needed to sell that airplane) without informing the second group of people about what had happened to those who had gone before.

This time, disaster struck. A sixty-year-old woman named Dorothy Miles, one of those senior citizens being paid $49 to take a ride down a slide, broke her neck going headfirst down an escape chute. She was left paralyzed from the neck down, one of twenty-one people injured in the second round of tests. The plane was evacuated in 112 seconds in round two, still too slow to get an FAA certification.

In the wake of these accidents, the FAA disclosed that some 5 to 10 percent of those involved in this kind of evacuation testing suffered broken bones or bruises, yet it defended using people to simulate full-scale real-world emergencies. The agency argued that there was no better way to find out if a plane was really safe.

But by 1993, the agency had apparently found a better way. It said that new procedures had been used to retest the MD-11. The changes included using phased tests of people's ability to get out, briefing them on what would be happening to them, and allowing test subjects to step out of the plane onto a raised platform instead of sliding to the ground below.

DISCARDED BY DECCA

A Decca Stacked Against the Beatles

The new year brings with it the hope for new beginnings, and so it was with a rock and roll quartet that called itself the Beatles on January 1, 1962.

The group had been called to audition for Decca Records in the American company's London studios. Several hundred miles from their home in Liverpool, John, Paul, George, and Pete Best (the drummer replaced by Ringo Starr later in the group's life) spent two hours strummin' and singin' fifteen songs.

The executives at Decca were underwhelmed. They were sure that four-piece groups were not the future of the music business, especially four-piece groups that played guitars. And the Beatles lived so far away. Where was the London-based talent?

So it was thumbs-down on the Beatles at Decca, and the rest, as they say, is music history.

When She Hesitated, and He Got Lost

In the world of high tech, the signing of nondisclosure agreements among parties that want to do business is as necessary as tea on an English breakfast table. But such documents are rarely controversial enough to prevent parties from coming together.

In the case of a company called Digital Research, however, failure to ink a nondisclosure document might have cost it billions of dollars, and a place in computer industry history. It all happened when Bill Gates approached the company with the idea of writing the operating software for a new computer IBM was developing.

Gates had called his old friend Gary Kildall at Digital Research and set up a fast meeting. IBM was in a hurry, and Gates wanted Kildall's company to write the new program.

But Kildall's wife, Dorothy McEwen, took care of all

the contracts for Digital Research, and it was she showed up for the meeting with the IBM people, not her husband. He was on an airplane to a business meeting somewhere else that day.

McEwen took a look at IBM's nondisclosure agreement and declared it virtually one-way enough to have a street named after it. The offending words in the document said the discussion that was about to take place between IBM and Digital Research would "not serve to impair the right of either party to make, procure, and market products or services now or in the future which may be competitive with those offered by the other."

McEwen saw those words as a license to take Digital Research's ideas and run with them. The meeting broke up and despite some further attempts to get the companies together, Gates went elsewhere for operating system software, eventually coming up with a program called DOS.

The DOS operating system was nothing less than the linchpin of Microsoft's astounding success story, putting the company literally at the base of operations of every IBM and IBM compatible PC.

All this success might have also come the way of Digital Research, if Gary Kildall hadn't taken a flier and Dorothy McEwen had lightened up the day IBM came calling.

STUCK WITH A BAD DEAL

For all those who have pinned their hopes on a new invention, the story of Walter Hunt is instructive. In 1849, Hunt found himself $15 in debt. Since he was broke and had few prospects, Hunt sat down with a pencil and paper and came up with a design for the safety pin.

The pin was a triumph of spontaneous innovation, but the business deal Hunt cut wasn't too sharp. He sold the rights to his creation for $400, thinking himself lucky to have made enough to pay off his debts and still have some walking around money left in his pockets.

A Rotten Core Decision at Apple Computer

In the annals of American entrepreneurial history, the saga of Apple Computer has a storied place. The company's founders, Steven Jobs and Steve Wozniak, came up with a new computer in their garage, got some venture capital backing, and built a company that took the high-tech world by storm. In 1984, Apple introduced its most famous product, the Macintosh computer, with a breakthrough ad on the Super Bowl that equated rival IBM and other computer makers with the Big Brother tyranny of George Orwell. It was a powerful message that positioned the Macintosh, according to *Business Week,* as "the very icon of a post-industrial, high-tech America."

Apple had built its success on a number of factors, but among them, perceived user friendliness might have been the most important. The Macintosh, with its mouse, icons, and point-and-click method of computing, polished Apple's image as the innovator in the world of computers on a desktop. But rather than conquer IBM and its competition, Apple's fortunes within a decade had soured to the point where it was becoming close to an also-ran in the microcomputer industry.

The company made many mistakes, but possibly its most damaging policy involved the attempt to keep Apple's technology proprietary. If Apple didn't make it, no one else would. Rather than license the Macintosh to clone makers on the eve of Microsoft's introduction of its Windows program in the late 1980s, Apple sat tight.

Microsoft's Windows worked a lot like Apple's Macintosh, with little icons and point-and-click facility. The imitation eroded Apple's reputation for innovation as well as its advantage in user friendliness. Suddenly, the premium prices Apple was charging for its allegedly more advanced systems looked high.

The seeds of decline had been sown, and the bloom was off the Apple blossom.

50

The Short Selling
of Superman

They made him faster than a speeding bullet, more powerful than a locomotive, and able to leap tall buildings at a single bound. But the teenagers who created the Man of Steel apparently didn't think enough of Superman to ask much money for him when it came time to sell the superhero to a comic book company.

Joe Schuster and Jerry Siegel reportedly received less than $200 when they sold Superman to D.C. Comics in 1938. To add injury to insult, the pair was fired in the 1940s for seeking an increase to the $10-a-page fee they were being paid to draw the comic.

Instead of becoming super-rich, the two men lived with little for years as they lost legal battles to win back the rights to their creation. Schuster worked as a messenger. Siegel was a clerk.

Finally, when Superman became a movie in 1978

and public opinion became important to Warner Bros., the movie company came up with $20,000 annual payments to Superman's real-life parents, which some said was really a payoff to keep quiet about what they had been through.

51

MA BELL'S
WRONG NUMBER

O nce upon a time, there was one telephone company that had a virtual monopoly on phone services in America. Its name was AT&T. But in 1984, a federal court order broke AT&T into pieces. The court carved the AT&T monolith into seven regional phone companies with monopolies on residential service. The AT&T that was left after the reorganization was a long-distance carrier banned from offering residential phone service but free to compete in almost any other business.

Among the most desirable businesses in AT&T's sights, computers ranked among the most luscious. AT&T would become a company that could meet any customer's need for both voice and data communications. It was an executive's dream, and the thinking seemed much more than magical.

Although AT&T had been restrained from selling computers by court decree since the mid-1950s, its corporate credentials in the computer field were pretty good. Bell Laboratories, the research arm of Ma Bell, had invented the transistor and had written the Unix operating system software. The company had produced computers for its internal use for a long time. Free at last to use its technological and financial muscle to build a position in the marketplace, AT&T set to work, with the goal of competing with IBM high on its "to do" list.

But you don't just shift overnight from a monopoly mentality to competition-savvy player, especially in the fast-paced world of high tech. From the start, little went right for AT&T in computers. Cost control was a problem. An industry downturn hurt sales. Within a couple of years, the new AT&T computer business was a $1 billion loser.

Joint ventures with Silicon Valley operations and foreign high-tech companies didn't fix things, but AT&T persisted. Some might suggest that the word for the motivations behind this decision is "hubris." Corporate myopia is another way to describe AT&T's doggedness. Or you could use a more politically correct euphemism such as "digitally challenged" to assess the AT&T position in the high-tech world.

In the early 1990s, the company appeared to decide that if it couldn't build its own success in the computer business, it would buy it. At a cost of about $7.5 billion, AT&T completed a hostile takeover of NCR, the Dayton, Ohio–based specialist in the manufacture of automated teller machines (ATMs) for banks and checkout sca. for grocery stores and other retailers.

It's been noted that trend is not necessarily destiny, but you couldn't say that about AT&T and computers. In a few short years, the folks at Ma Bell were probably wishing for the good old early days of computer failure.

Far from the success that planners had hoped for, NCR turned out to be the most troubled venture yet. Chief executive officers came and went yearly. By 1995, the new AT&T division was reportedly losing $2 million a day. One commentator called the deal "among the worst since God invented money."

Just how bad was that? In September 1995, AT&T announced it was splitting itself into three pieces. The computer part of its operations would become a separate company with a publicly traded stock. By the middle of 1997, the market value of that new company's stock was about $3.3 billion, or less than half of what AT&T paid for NCR in 1991.

WELL-EARNED WRENCH

52

A WRENCHING LOSS FOR SEARS

When Sears executives in Chicago saw the plans for a new quick-release socket wrench sent in by a teenager working for the company in a Massachusetts store, there was immediate interest. Amazing but true, the company suggestion box had produced what looked like a possible winner.

But instead of finding the innovative young employee and making him an example of how Sears rewards initiative, creativity, and loyalty with praise and a handsome payment, the company behaved quite differently. It told Peter Roberts that his invention, which allowed car mechanics and others to change sockets with just one hand, didn't have much sales potential. The wrench would be expensive to produce, Sears said, and unless Sears spent lots of money to advertise it, there would be few buyers. The company estimated sales potential at fifty thousand a year, if that.

In a letter to Roberts seeking patent rights to the wrench, Sears offered $10,000. Sears made the paltry offer when it had actually determined that the wrench was an excellent product that mechanics especially liked, that it could be produced at a low cost and sold for a handsome profit.

The wrench became a best-seller for Sears, with some nineteen million sold between 1965 and 1975.

These facts came out in a series of court battles between Roberts and Sears that lasted almost a decade. The Supreme Court ultimately handed Sears a wrenching defeat for its treatment of Roberts, awarding him a $1 million judgment.

53

THE HEAVY COST OF PORTABLE SUCCESS

The laptop computer is a ubiquitous status symbol of the 1990s, and it's brought big profits to companies like IBM, Toshiba, Dell, Compaq, Apple, and others with popular models. But you won't find the name Osborne Computers among the ranks of the long-term laptop winners, even though Osborne brought the first portable computer to market in the early 1980s, and it was an almost overnight success.

The Osborne I weighed twenty-five pounds, and the heavy lift was a small deterrent to business people hungry for a machine they could take along on trips.

The computer's creator, Adam Osborne, had designed a system with everything you needed to take care of business away from the office. It had two floppy disk drives, system software, word processing, and a database that allowed users to get to work as soon as they could plug in the machine. The price was right, too. At

$1,795, you could put an Osborne I on your credit card and pay later—a strong incentive to impulse buyers that Adam Osborne was hoping for and got.

The whole package of product and price generated enormous demand, one problem that Adam Osborne was not prepared to deal with successfully. He had built a better mousetrap, but he had failed, as analysts of the Osborne experience have noted, to build a better mousetrap company.

There was early and effective competition to the Osborne I. Some of the technology that the Osborne used was fast becoming obsolete, and by 1983, less than two years after its smashing early success with Osborne I, the company declared bankruptcy.

54

A Poorly Krafted Promotion

The first paragraph of the story in *The Wall Street Journal* of August 23, 1991, pretty much said it all:

A bungled cheese promotion that was supposed to cost Kraft USA $63,000 in prizes will instead cost it $10 million to settle a class action lawsuit, filed on behalf of thousands of customers who thought they had won the grand prize.

And how did Kraft turn a low-budget promotion designed to enhance sales of its Kraft Singles cheese into a legal nightmare that offended thousands and wound up costing millions? Not without lots of effort.

The promotion in question was called "Ready to Roll." It was pretty simple. Consumers were asked to match game pieces they found in the cheese packages with game pieces printed in Sunday newspaper fliers.

If you were lucky enough to "match" the one half of a minivan you found in a cheese package with the other half of the minivan you found in the Sunday newspaper, the $17,000 vehicle was yours.

Kraft planned to give away only one minivan as the grand prize in the promotion, along with one hundred bicycles, five hundred skateboards, and eight thousand packages of cheese. But a printing bungle turned out thousands of matches, and, incredibly, no one at Kraft caught the mistake before the product packaging and newspaper fliers were distributed.

Some ten thousand people claimed they had winning matches for minivans. In all, there were reportedly some two million potential winners of some kind in Chicago and Houston, where the promotion was run.

Not surprisingly, Kraft declared the promotion null and void immediately, and the company didn't go into details about what had happened, saying only that a printing error had occurred. It also announced a plan to award $250 to each "winner" of the grand prize van and to give all ten thousand big prize claimants a shot to win one of four minivans at a later drawing.

Of course, the skimpy explanation was received as an attempt to welch on the promotion by an angry public. There was enough anger to generate the class-action suit that Kraft ultimately settled at a cost no one could possibly have imagined when someone came up with the bright idea known as "Ready to Roll." Usually a whiz at cheese marketing, Kraft had sliced it too thin this time.

55

THE POST OFFICE
GOES BACK TO THE FUTURE

Brilliant, competent, efficient, polite, and visionary are not adjectives often used to describe the United States Postal Service. After all, this *is* the organization that has seen its employees go crazy and open fire with guns, adding the phrase "going postal" to the lexicon of madness. And it is the post office that spent more than $6 million in the 1990s to change its logo from an eagle to an eagle.

So it's not surprising that a plan to put the post office into the on-line world has been causing some raised eyebrows. It's especially puzzling since the post office said no to electronic links more than two decades ago when it was offered a connection to ARPAnet, the Pentagon-developed data-carrying web that ultimately became the Internet.

Now, the cyberstrategy of the nation's mail carrier includes offering electronic "postmarking" of documents

131

as a way to prove the time and date a message was transmitted and that it was not tampered with. The target market is law firms, government agencies, financial institutions, and others with a need to know exactly when a court filing, competitive bid, or other time-verifiable document was delivered.

Of course, the service will be somewhat slower than regular E-mail, and there will be extra charges involved for electronic postmarking. It does put another player in the document transmission stream, a complication that could create the chance for delivery mistakes. And if the idea seems to be a good one, it's inevitable that competition will spring up—competition that has bedeviled the post office in businesses like package delivery.

Nonetheless, there's a bullish attitude on cyberspace projects at Uncle Sam's mail carrier in the 1990s, with little thought about what might have been had a similar decision been taken in the 1970s.

56

OH BABY,
WHAT A JUICY SCAM

Did you have a baby between 1978 and 1982? Did your pride and joy like to drink apple juice during those years? Was the Beech-Nut brand a particular favorite?

If you answered yes to those three questions, you will most likely be surprised to know that it wasn't apple juice at all that your offspring was sipping. That's because there was no apple juice at all in the Beech-Nut product during those years. In an attempt to save money and boost profits, Beech-Nut put an apple-juice-free product on the shelves, and labeled it "100 percent" pure apple juice.

Employees of the company thought something was fishy because of the huge price break Beech-Nut was getting on apple juice concentrate, and it didn't take long for them to understand that the "apple juice" they were producing was totally bogus. Nonetheless, the bottling machines went on filling, and the trucks rolled out with cases of the stuff destined for the shopping carts of America's brand-trusting mothers and the tender palates of the nation's infants and toddlers.

In fact, the drink was nothing much more than a mix of water, sugar, and flavorings. One Beech-Nut executive referred to it as little more than a chemical cocktail. By any name, it was a consumer fraud of unparalleled proportions and among the most jaw-dropping examples of executive idiocy imaginable.

The despicable deceit was eventually unearthed by some sleuthing on behalf of a trade association that suspected hanky-panky by the supplier of apple juice concentrate that Beech-Nut was using to make the drink. It involved real detective work that included cloak and dagger–style searches through Dumpsters at night and the trailing of a truck loaded with phony apple juice concentrate to the scene of the bottling crime.

The wrongdoing brought Beech-Nut a $2 million fine from the federal government for a 215-count violation of the Food, Drug and Cosmetic Act—the largest such levy ever—and it put two top Beech-Nut executives into criminal court on consumer fraud charges. Niels Hoyvald, the former president of Beech-Nut, and John Lavery, a vice president, were both found guilty, fined $100,000, and sentenced to prison terms of a year and a day.

And how did the crime pay? It's been estimated that the bogus concentrate never saved Beech-Nut more than $250,000 a year in an annual apple juice manufacturing budget of about $50 million. That's a yearly cost saving of about one half of one percent. Measure that against the damage done to Beech-Nut's credibility by its apparent breaching of what is possibly society's most inviolable taboo—the welfare of children—and you get a feel for how well Messrs. Hoyvald and Lavery understood the cost of everything and the value of nothing.

57

IBM DOSn't Get It

O f all the deals in the history of high tech, IBM's decision to licence the DOS operating system from Microsoft for its first personal computer might possibly be the most significant. The program that eventually became known as MS-DOS was legendary for its success in helping to build Microsoft into the corporate colossus it has become. So how come IBM didn't buy the system outright, or write operating software of its own that would be proprietary?

In developing its personal computer in 1980, IBM faced a tight schedule. Top executives wanted to see a machine fast. Managers on the project faced classic build-or-buy decisions, but with no time to start from scratch, they hit the road with their checkbooks.

When it came to the need for an operating system, the key interface between a computer's hardware and the application programs such as word processing and spreadsheets that do things for users, Bill Gates and Microsoft was the place to go shopping. But the shrewd Gates wasn't selling anything outright.

Anticipating the cloning of IBM's machine, he decided it was in Microsoft's best interests to license an operating system to IBM, but keep the ability to license the same product to companies that were building machines that were similar to IBM's.

So IBM's deal with Gates was a rental, not a buy.

As almost anyone whose fingers have ever caressed a computer keyboard knows by now, the MS-DOS deal with IBM made Microsoft's operating system the personal computer industry standard, with IBM and every other company making IBM compatible computers putting the operating system in its machines and paying Microsoft for the right to do it.

58

NBC's *DATELINE:*
BLOWN CREDIBILITY

In the landmark mid-1970s film *Network,* writer Paddy Chayefsky painted an outrageously entertaining satirical portrait of a network news operation that played hard for ratings by doing almost anything to win an audience, except practicing honest, but sometimes boring, journalism.

It seemed that this value system had infected NBC's *Dateline* newsmagazine years later when it was disclosed that producers and reporters had not played fair and square in reporting on the alleged safety problems of a GM truck.

An analysis of the videotape of a two-truck test crash revealed the *Dateline* broadcast had failed to disclose that a sparking device had been attached to the bottom of one of the trucks. While it remains disputed whether that device was the cause of a fire that resulted from the crash, there was no question that the NBC News people had strayed from the accepted norms of journalism in their failure to disclose.

It seemed that *Dateline* was more interested in guaranteeing pictures of a crash and fire than in letting its cameras record what might have happened without any potential technical enhancements.

GM cried a loud "foul." Some models of the truck *Dateline* was investigating had exploded on collision, and there were some legitimate questions about safety, but the *Dateline* "test" could hardly be called fair.

NBC wound up apologizing for its momentary lapse of integrity, ending one of the sorriest chapters in the long-running story of a very distinguished news organization.

A VACUUS PLAN

59

A Free Lesson
for Hoover

Sometimes you just have to leap before you look, but there was nothing so urgent that executives at Hoover, the vacuum cleaner manufacturer, couldn't have spent a little more time thinking through a promotion that blew sky-high.

The scheme seemed like a great way to increase vacuum cleaner sales: Just give buyers free airline tickets with the purchase of a new vacuum cleaner.

But when the idea was tried in British and Irish stores, Hoover discovered it was flying in uncharted territory. One deal offered two free airline tickets worth up to $600 with each vacuum cleaner purchase of $150 or more. A second offering promised a pair of round-trip tickets to New York or Orlando to those buying at least $375 worth of Hoover products.

The offers took off to the tune of more than 200,000

consumers buying into the free tickets deal. It all added up to an award of 400,000 round-trip tickets (one for every 150 people who lived in Great Britain and Ireland in the early 1990s) and almost $50 million in losses for Hoover.

Postmortems of the costly miscue noted that, unlike Hoover vacuum cleaners, this was one promotion that suffered from extremely poor design.

60

THANKS A LOT

W e're sure Neiman Marcus, the upscale department store, had all the best intentions when it sent special thank-you notes to big-ticket jewelry customers. It was, after all, an exceedingly polite thing to do, and it seemed like a nice way to maintain customer loyalty, as well.

It hardly worked out that way.

Most of the notes were addressed to men, the people who had paid for the expensive baubles. But most of the envelopes were opened by women. Unfortunately for Neiman Marcus, too many of these women—wives of the purchasers mostly—had not been the recipients of the costly purchases.

Many of the gaudy gifts had gone to mistresses, and Neiman Marcus had unintentionally blown the whistle.

Neiman Marcus might have avoided its faux pas by

talking to people at United Airlines. Years earlier United ran a promotion intended to induce businessmen to take their wives along on business trips. The famous "Take Me Along" campaign did produce lots of new couples in the friendly skies, but many of them weren't married.

61

Commercial Videotex: On Line but Off Target

L ong before the Internet and WorldWideWeb were making on-line information technology the darling of Wall Street and the subject of endless cocktail party chatter, some of America's most prestigious media and communications companies were losing small fortunes trying to commercialize a system known as Videotex.

Videotex did many of the things you can do today with a personal computer and a modem: find out the latest news, get up-to-the-minute sports scores, check stock prices, look at weather forecasts, play games, make airline reservations, order lots of different kinds of products, and other allegedly wonderful things. The technology you needed for Videotex might sound familiar—a monitor and keyboard, a terminal and a modem for your telephone. The idea was you would buy the technology from a Videotex provider, and then also pay user fees when you used the system's offerings.

In the early 1980s, Knight-Ridder, Times Mirror, CBS, IBM, AT&T, and others all took a serious crack at making commercial Videotex work. How much did these media giants invest in this ultimate loser? Estimates have varied and there are no definitive statistics, but more than $500 million is probably on the low side. Knight-Ridder alone is reported to have lost $60 million.

There were lots of reasons Videotex didn't work, many of them seemingly quite obvious and potentially applicable to today's information highway and some of the more highly touted applications.

First of all, the economics of Videotex were difficult. Consumers were asked to shell out as much as $600 for the hardware to get the service and then pay additional monthly fees and special charges for use. You could use Videotex only for data retrieval or some interactive function that the system permitted. It was not a personal computer, with word processing, spreadsheet, and other applications. You couldn't fax to or from Videotex, and the databases to which it had access were quite limited.

Another problem was that Videotex was a clumsy way to do many of the things it was supposed to do best. Books and newspapers were more efficient ways to find things out, and you could carry them from room to room. Catalogs were better for shopping. People don't really like to read a glowing screen, and Videotex did not have the sound and video of today's digital systems.

146

The power of Videotex was that it provided up-to-the-minute information on just about anything. But that wasn't enough to make it a success. In the end, the commercial hopes for Videotex foundered on realities of the marketplace that even lay observers found hard to ignore.

62

A Tale That's
Hard to Bear

There's no such thing as a stock market, say the Wall
Street wags, there's only a market of stocks.

It's important to remember this when making investment decisions, but most of us don't have the disci-
pline. We want to know about the great shifts in the
market as a whole. Is it going up or down? When and
by how much? Is now a good time to invest?

To answer questions like these, Wall Street has no shortage of opinion mavens who predict coming events based on
analytical techniques and theories that employ everything
from the highest mathematics to astrology. These folks are
called bulls and bears, colorfully named after the animal
spirits that are said to motivate investors and move markets.

But don't make the mistake of betting your pension
on the prophesies of any one of these pundits. Despite
their theories, track records, and carefully made argu-
ments, they can be almost laughably wrong. There are

lots of examples, but possibly none as colorful or instructive as the case of Joe Granville.

Joe Granville had a place in the sun as a market timer for a while in the early 1980s. His predictions of where the market was going were so uncannily correct, that his calls became front page-news. Granville became so influential in the fate of the markets he was quoted as saying he had four times the power of the Federal Reserve to influence stock prices.

People clamored to hear and see him. He sold out investment seminars that had whiz-bang show-biz effects as well as market advice. There were costumes, balloons, and women in bikinis, with Joe Granville as the ringmaster in the investment circus.

But the music stopped for Granville in 1982, when he became a market bear. He told investors to sell stocks at precisely the time that prices had reached lows that would not be seen again. The Great Bull Market of the 1980s had begun with Joe Granville on the wrong side of the stock market–timing fence. In August 1982, when the Dow Jones Industrial Average dropped under 780, Granville predicted any rallies from that point would be fast and fizzling. He saw stocks going lower.

But they didn't, and nothing Granville could say would make them go down. While Granville clung to his bearish views, the Dow Jones average would more than triple in the next five years. Joe Granville, who had so confidently predicted he would win the Nobel Prize for his acumen, lost most of his credibility, and the bulk of his investment following.

63

THEIR TRUTH BROUGHT CONSEQUENCES

Quiz shows in the 1950s were a national craze. The super-brainy contestants on programs such as *The $64,000 Question* and *Twenty-One* became national celebrities thanks to their astounding range and depth of knowledge and feats of memory under pressure. Millions sat on the edges of their living room sofas waiting anxiously for people like Charles Van Doren to come up with the right answer and win enormous sums of money.

It was engaging entertainment that sure kept an audience's interest. Here was a fabulous formula that had all the elements of dramatic success. There was suspense and humor, heroes and villains, winners and losers all wrapped together in an admirable package of intellect and achievement. Just turn on the lights, check the ratings, and collect the sponsor's money.

But that wasn't quite good enough for the producers

of these high-profile entertainments. Or maybe they should be called the "overproducers." To make sure that there was enough drama and that the most appealing winners stayed on TV, they fed answers to selected contestants, and coached them on how to deliver them in the most credible and telegenic way.

Their cheatin' hearts were ultimately revealed when some contestants blew the whistle on the fakery. The quiz show scandals of the 1950s became the best television going. There were winners and losers, heroes and villains, here too. Somehow, it wasn't quite so entertaining to watch the squirmings of a lot of smart people who had done some very stupid things.

64

A PINHEADED MAILING

In 1994, NYNEX sent all of its phone credit card hold-ers a notice in the mail urging them to use their call-ing cards to qualify for a promotional sweepstakes.

The mailing brought an instant and intense reaction that wasn't triggered by the promotion. People were in-censed to find their supposedly superconfidential calling credit card Personal Identification Number (PIN) printed on the mailing label for all to see and for the unethical to use.

What was such a private number doing in such a public place? It was quite a shift from the sealed enve-lope used to send the PIN to card holders.

Oops, said the phone company, swiftly sending all its phone credit card customers an important information flash. Not to worry, said the damage control communi-qué, new PIN numbers would be sent around shortly and customers wouldn't be charged for any unauthorized calls that might show up on their bills.

Possibly hoping that actions would speak louder than words, phone company execs in the aftermath of the mess seemed reluctant to recognize the full measure of the snafu, with one marketing executive reportedly sniffing that "there are always ways to improve a program."

65

THE GOOSE THAT COOKED HOWARD HUGHES

The year was 1942. The world was at war, and the Atlantic Ocean was a killing zone for Germany's deadly U-boats.

In an attempt to end the terror on the high seas, two distinguished businessmen hatched an idea that was enormously appealing: build a kind of flying boat that could whisk men and supplies over the Atlantic far above Germany's marauding U-boats and help the allies win World War II.

It was the shared brainchild of shipping magnate Henry J. Kaiser and the legendary Howard Hughes. The airplane was formally christened the *HK-1*, but it quickly got the nickname the "Spruce Goose," because it was to be built almost entirely out of wood.

The sobriquet was a misnomer that Hughes is said to have detested. The plane was, in fact, to be built mostly out of birch. To a press corps looking for good copy,

"Birch Goose" didn't come quite so trippingly off the tongue, and wasn't one wood pretty much the same as another, anyway? Hughes's perfectionism about the relatively harmless inaccuracy, however, was an indicator of obsessions to come.

The seaplane was designed to carry sixty tons of cargo. It would be the largest plane ever built, much larger than today's huge 747 aircraft. There was a big rush on the project from the War Department. It wanted the first three prototypes in the air within a year of the start of work. There were visions of an annual production of five hundred flying boats whisking men and material to the war effort against Germany and Japan.

But Howard Hughes was the caricature of the hands-on manager, and he obsessed over even the smallest details of the plane. He wanted special trees for certain parts, so there were extensive searches for the right woods throughout the U.S. and Canada. He paid personal attention to individual nuts and bolts before they could be installed.

Meanwhile, the war wound on. Eventually, the federal government stopped paying for the plane, and Kaiser pulled out of the partnership. Hughes, however, persevered, pumping his own money into the project.

World War II ended in victory for the Allies without any help from the Spruce Goose. The first model was still being built, and there were lots of questions about whether the behemoth would even fly.

The Spruce Goose did not make a maiden flight until

156

nearly a year after the war was over. One day in 1947, Hughes did take his obsession out for a sixty-second spin over the Long Beach harbor in California. The airplane didn't go very fast, only about sixty miles an hour, and it didn't get very high in the sky.

No one ever flew the plane again. What had started as a noble effort to save lives and end a terrible war had become one of the modern era's most fascinating total failures.

HERB: BURGER KING'S RARE WHOPPER

Like hostesses who worry about giving parties that too few people attend, marketing execs fret about ad campaigns that everyone will hate.

So with so much advance (though not necessarily advanced) thinking, the appearance of the roundly detested Herb as a promoter for Burger King in the mid-1980s is a real head scratcher. How could such a shrewd marketer of fast food come up with such a whopping promotional mistake?

Not without lots of effort.

Herb was a nerdy character who was supposed to be the only person in America who had never tasted a Whopper. Hoping to stimulate consumer curiosity, Burger King talked Herb up for months, but never actually showed him until a commercial during the 1986 Super Bowl telecast.

As a follow-up to Herb's debut on national television,

Burger King offered cash prizes of $5,000 to first sighters of Herb at some store promotions.

In total, Burger King spent $40 million on the Herb campaign, with the result that the fast-food giant's popularity actually decreased. Researchers told Burger King that people were either annoyed with Herb or, possibly worse, just bored by him.

67

THEY WENT BANANAS AT SILO

Maybe because we need it to live, we use lots of foods to substitute for the word "money" when we talk. Beans, cabbage, lettuce, and coconuts all stand in for the "m" word from time to time.

So it's probable that the people at Silo, a consumer electronics discounter, thought that everyone would "get it" when they advertised a promotion in the mid-1980s offering a stereo for the low, low price of "299 bananas."

People in Seattle and El Paso, where the deal was offered in a TV commercial, got it, all right. Or rather, we should say, got Silo.

Lined up outside Silo stores, people brought bags of bananas to cash in for the stereos. The banana slip cost Silo more than $10,000 in merchandise for fruit transactions, allowing Silo execs the tasty pleasure of, literally, eating their words.

161

FOUL PLAY

A Home Run Idea That Struck Out

Is there a more American combination than baseball and Coca-Cola? Chances are the folks at the Coca-Cola bottler in Cookeville, Tennessee, didn't think so when they planned a sales-building promotion that married the sport to the beverage.

Under the rules of the "Home Run" contest, bottle caps were produced with letters embossed inside them. Consumers who had bottle caps with the letters that spelled out the words "home run" would win prizes.

To limit the number of prize winners, only a few letter R's were to be produced. But more than eighteen thousand more R's than the bottler planned for eventually wound up inside bottle caps. So much for quality control.

The misprinting cost more than $100,000 in unintended prize awards before company execs put a final cap on the game.

GTE Gets
All Shook Up

An earthquake in Southern California left the billing records of GTE, the phone company, all shook up for January 17, 1994.

That was Martin Luther King Day nationally, but GTE didn't recognize it as a holiday for billing discount purposes. On holidays it did recognize, like the Fourth of July and Christmas, callers got 60 percent off usual rates. But earthquakes do funny things and this time one of the postquake quirks turned out to be mistaken reductions in GTE customers' phone bills for January 17.

Not that GTE noticed. It took a call from an honest customer reporting an undercharge to alert the company to the mistake it had made. It took four months for GTE to get out new bills to recoup the estimated $1.5 million in losses from the mistakenly discounted Martin Luther King Day calls.

But the delay put GTE beyond the California ninety-day limit for back billing, triggering charges of a rip-off attempt and insensitivity for not giving discounts on King's birthday.

So an initial error of commission was followed by a customer-corrected error of omission that brought another error of commission, all of which wound up with GTE granting the discount and taking the $1.5 million loss, which is where we got on this bus in the first place.

70

DONE DEALS, DUMB DEALS:
BASEBALL

Success in professional team sports depends on lots of factors. Coaching, management, facilities, schedules, injuries, luck, and money all play their parts. But if you want to win, you must first and foremost have the best players. There are several ways to get superior personnel. You can trade for the right stuff with another team. Or you can buy players, or draft them. The question is, what's the right stuff? The pursuit of the answer has produced some deals that sports fans still talk about for their essential idiocy, although all the transactions certainly must have seemed like good ideas at the time.

Among American sports icons, possibly none has the staying power of George Herman "Babe" Ruth—the Bambino, the Sultan of Swat. Who hasn't seen the newsreel footage of him trotting around the bases in his New York Yankee pinstripes after another prodigious home run?

In Boston, such images are especially galling. This is

because Babe Ruth played for the Red Sox in his early career, helping Boston win the World Series in 1915, 1916, and 1918. But in 1920, Ruth was sold to the Yankees for something like $100,000 (the figure is disputed). Harry Frazee, the Red Sox owner, used the dough to finance production of the musical *No, No, Nanette* on Broadway.

No, No, Nanette became a hit, but the musical's success couldn't come close to matching the heights the Yankees scaled with the Babe in their lineup. In his fifteen seasons with the team, the Bronx Bombers won seven American League pennants and four World Series.

Without George Herman Ruth, the Red Sox went on to legendary frustration—through the 1996 season, no Boston team has ever won a World Series.

The Cincinnati Reds hadn't done much winning before Frank Robinson joined their club in 1956. The gifted outfielder won Rookie of the Year honors that year, immediately making the Reds a team to be reckoned with.

In 1961, Robinson was named the Most Valuable Player in the National League, leading Cincinnati to a pennant and the team's first World Series appearance since 1940. And although the Reds lost that year to the Yankees, Robinson had become one of the premier players in baseball. A home run threat with every trip to the plate, he was a hitter in the same class as Hank Aaron, Willie Mays, Mickey Mantle, Ernie Banks, Stan Musial, and other Hall of Famers of that era.

So it was with some surprise that baseball fans greeted the news that Frank Robinson, at age thirty, was being traded from Cincinnati to the Baltimore Orioles for the 1966 season. "Too old," said Cincinnati management, who welcomed the left-handed pitcher, Milt Pappas, to the Queen City on the Ohio River in return for the allegedly aging star outfielder.

History records that in 1966, the Baltimore Orioles won the World Series, with the "too old" Frank Robinson named Most Valuable Player in the American League that year. Although a candidate for a geriatric ward by Cincinnati standards, Robinson batted .316, drove in 122 runs, and smacked 49 home runs during the regular season to pace the Orioles and win the American League Triple Crown.

In 1970, Frank Robinson and the Baltimore Orioles defeated the Cincinnati Reds in the World Series. Robinson stayed with the Orioles through 1971, ending his career as an active player in 1976—a decade after Cincinnati declared him over the hill.

To date, Frank Robinson is the only major leaguer ever to win Most Valuable Player honors in both leagues. He became baseball's first African-American manager in 1975, when he took the helm of the Cleveland Indians as a player/manager. In 1982, Frank Robinson was elected to baseball's Hall of Fame on the first ballot.

DONE DEALS, DUMB DEALS:
FOOTBALL

The growth of the National Football League (NFL) is one of America's fascinating business success stories. From a second-rate attraction in the 1950s, the NFL has mushroomed into an international sports and entertainment juggernaut. Once upon a time, there was actually no such thing as a Super Bowl. Now, the annual football rite has become a de facto national holiday. Super Bowl broadcasts clutter the list of most-watched television programs of all time.

Among the owners of NFL football teams, the lust for a Super Bowl trophy is especially deep. Nowhere is this ache more heartfelt than in the executive suites of the Minnesota Vikings. Through thirty-one Super Bowls, the Vikings had been to what is referred to as "the Big Show" four times and never won.

What was the missing ingredient of ultimate success? In 1989, the Vikings decided that a world-class running back was the final piece in their championship puzzle. To find one, they looked south to Texas, where a Heisman Trophy winner named Herschel Walker wore the silver, white, and blue uniform of the Dallas Cowboys.

Walker was big, fast and strong—just the game breaker Minnesota needed, or so the Vikings reasoning went. To get him, they gave the Cowboys five players and seven future draft picks. The draft choices included three first-round picks, three second-round choices, and one third-round pick. All together, Minnesota was giving Dallas more than a full team for just one player.

The deal left lots of football experts wondering whether Minnesota's executives had taken leave of their senses, and Vikings General Manager Mike Lynn acknowledged the risk in noting that the team might be mortgaging its future in the hope for quick success. But Lynn's worst nightmares probably didn't rival what actually came to pass as a result of the deal, which some wags quickly labeled the "Great Train Robbery."

Within three years of the trade, it was Dallas, not Minnesota, that was winning the Super Bowl. And it was the Cowboys, not the Vikings, that got the running back who brought championships as a result of the swap.

The Herschel Walker deal brought to the Cowboys a running back named Emmitt Smith from the University of Florida. Smith's fluid style, power, and work ethic helped bring Super Bowl titles to Dallas in 1993, 1994, and 1996. With Walker, the Vikings didn't come close to championship glory, and by 1991, Herschel was cut by the team, which didn't think his on-field performance merited his million-dollar-plus annual salary.

The Herschel Walker deal will go down in sports history as one of the worst personnel decisions ever made by a sports franchise, but was it the absolute worst? This is the stuff of great debates among sports fans, and there are lots of other examples that, with the advantage of twenty-twenty hindsight, can be cited as all-time great screwups.

For example, in the 1984 NBA draft of college basketball talent, both the Houston Rockets and Portland Trail Blazers used first-round picks to take seven-foot centers. Houston's pick, Hakeem Olajuwon, became one of the game's great stars, leading the Rockets to consecutive NBA titles in the 1990s. Portland's choice, Sam Bowie, never made it big.

In making its decision, Portland rejected a graceful jump shooter from the University of North Carolina whose aerial exploits seemed to defy gravity. And so, with the third selection in the 1984 NBA draft, the Chicago Bulls chose Michael Jordan.

72

DR. TALLER'S DIET SHORTCUT

D r. Herman Taller's specialty was obstetrics and gynecology, so he had an up-close and personal view of the famous estimate that there's a sucker born every minute.

Whether this might have been the genesis of his unorthodox idea that caloric intake was not an important variable in weight loss is an interesting speculation, but it's no matter of conjecture that Taller's reducing ideas included the notion that you could eat five thousand calories a day.

This fat-headed fiction was included in Taller's bestselling book entitled *Calories Don't Count*. It was a tempting tome for the credulous, suggesting it was possible to lose weight while eating lots of fried foods and never leaving the table hungry.

Taller maintained that it wasn't how little you ate that took off the pounds, but what proportion of fats, proteins, and carbohydrates you consumed. He said all you had to do to shed that unwanted adipose was to eat the right stuff in the right mix, and take two special little pills with every meal.

The pills were named CDC capsules ("Calories Don't Count"), and the idea was that they contained a discovery that helped the body burn fat faster. What they actually contained was safflower oil, hardly a proven fat fighter, and the FDA rushed to get a court order to stop their sale on the grounds that the CDC capsules would never deliver the complete and undeniably alluring range of benefits they promised. These included a better sex life, fewer colds, a better complexion, lower cholesterol, and less heartburn. Oh well, at least they didn't promise to make you rich.

Maybe that's why Dr. Taller was convicted on only twelve of forty-nine counts of mail fraud, conspiracy, and violating the Federal Food, Drug and Cosmetics Act in 1967. His light sentence was just desserts: two years probation and a fine of just $7,000.

73

REACH FOR THE SKY
AT TCI

The request seemed ordinary enough. The woman said her car had broken down and she needed to use the phone. So the guard at TCI Cablevision in Tulsa, Oklahoma, one evening in March 1993 let her into the office complex, triggering some quite extraordinary events.

Once through the door, the woman pulled a semiautomatic pistol and was followed closely by a man with a revolver. He grabbed a female employee, put a gun to her head, and demanded money.

People were sure they were about to die, but it was over almost as soon as it had started. The holdup was a fake.

This was a mock break-in staged by their employer in the interests of their safety—an unwanted fringe benefit designed to teach employees what to do in case of a real emergency. The whole thing was real enough to unhinge several supervisors who knew what was coming.

Four workers sued, charging that TCI had assaulted them with a deadly weapon and intentionally subjected them to emotional stress. Had stupidity been in the criminal code, it's likely several counts would have been included in their complaint.

74

Privacy Is Right:
How Lexis-Nexis Learned

Its name is a little peculiar, but its service is very powerful. That power is why Lexis-Nexis, the on-line database company, has been so successful over the years. But a feature of its P-Trak Person Locator database service showing individual Social Security numbers turned out to be a powerful source of criticism.

P-Trak debuted in June 1996 with names, birthdays, current and former addresses, telephone numbers, and other information on people who had applied for credit. The target market for this data was said to be lawyers who often need to find witnesses and defendants, missing beneficiaries, and pensioners.

The inclusion of Social Security numbers brought a hail of complaints from people charging violation of privacy.

It didn't take long for Lexis-Nexis to take those complaints seriously and pull Social Security numbers off its screens. Within eleven days, the company had implemented the change, noting that Social Security numbers would remain a part of a person's record in its system but would no longer be included automatically in information that was displayed.

While it does seem somewhat dim for a company as sophisticated as Lexis-Nexis to have made such sensitive data so easily available, some privacy experts have suggested the dimwits might, in fact, be the complainers. They note that Social Security numbers are not exactly secrets, with people routinely putting them on job applications and that some states even require them on driver's licenses.

75

PowerMaster:
Off-Target Marketing

Target marketing is a time-honored technique, but sometimes you can really shoot yourself in the foot. So you might have expected a little more savvy and sensitivity from the G. Heileman Brewing Company when it decided to extend its line of Colt 45 malt liquors in 1991 with a new brew dubbed PowerMaster.

The suspect suds were almost 6 percent alcohol, much higher than regular beer, and even more potent than Colt 45. The problem was that malt liquors like PowerMaster are mostly consumed by African Americans, and it seemed to some that Heileman's new product was designed to increase the rate of drunkenness and alcoholism among them. Why would people think such a thing? Maybe it was because of the ads showing happy, successful African Americans that Heileman brewed up to sell the product.

There were screams of protest against PowerMaster

and prejudice at G. Heileman Brewing from black activists, industry leaders, federal officials, and the media. This had happened before when R. J. Reynolds had targeted black smokers with a new cigarette called Uptown. Even McDonald's had been criticized for hotly pursuing poor blacks with high-fat, high-sodium fast-food pitches, but these lessons had apparently been lost on Heileman in its product planning.

Just a few weeks after its introduction, Heileman pulled the plug on PowerMaster.

76

THE WHICH HUNT
AT PROCTER & GAMBLE

No company likes to read its secrets—dirty little, proprietary product, strategic planning, or any other kind—in the newspapers. But any time you have more than one person in a room, you've got an information control problem that's serious. And since a unilateral corporate decision is about as common as a chicken with lips, you might have thought executives at Procter & Gamble would have handled a few newspaper leaks with more equanimity.

Au contraire.

In June 1991, the company used a subpoena and the help of Cincinnati police in an attempt to find out who had slipped some of P&G's proprietary information to *The Wall Street Journal.* The company examined the phone records of a reported eight hundred thousand people in the Cincinnati area trying to find the culprit. Was there any chance that P&G would find the unauthorized talker before word got out about what it was doing to find the leaker?

Pas du tout.

Quickly, a tide of protest rolled in that was $99^{44}/100$ percent purely condemnatory of P&G's apparent disregard of a person's right to privacy, even if it was seeking to protect its own corporate right to keep secrets. There was scorn from the press, which labeled P&G's top brass bullies, determined bunglers, and other unflattering names. Worse, there were suggestions that, whatever benefit P&G might derive from stanching the unauthorized information flow, it risked losing more in the court of public opinion than any disclosed trade secret might turn out to be worth.

Admitting that its chosen cure was probably worse than the wound, P&G hung up its phone search.

77

WHEN PIZZA HUT HELD MORE THAN THE ANCHOVIES

They were proud of the Paseo Academy School of the Fine and Performing Arts in Kansas City, Missouri. It was a model of the city's desegregation program. So civic tempers were especially hot when it was revealed that Pizza Hut had refused delivery of $450 worth of food to the school. It was no everyday order Pizza Hut said no to. Those pizzas were supposed to be the main course for a student honor luncheon.

The incident was especially stupefying because Pizza Hut was angling for a $170,000 food delivery contract with the Kansas City Board of Education at the same time it was keeping its distance from Paseo on grounds that the neighborhood the school was in was too dangerous for its drivers.

Under proposed terms of that agreement, Pizza Hut would send pizza to twenty-one schools in Kansas City during the school year, and one of them was Paseo.

Pizza Hut won the delivery deal, but several days after the announcement, news of the Paseo delivery snub canceled the contract.

In discussing its cheesy performance in the media, a Pizza Hut spokesman appeared not to want to say no again. Yes, he answered, the company had made a mistake in refusing delivery to Paseo. Yes, the neighborhood around the school was unsafe for its drivers. Yes, if a future order came from Paseo, Pizza Hut would deliver.

The whole issue is probably academic, however. Students at Paseo have long since given Pizza Hut an F.

78

HUBBLE TROUBLES

The images from the Hubble space telescope have allowed scientists to penetrate many of the mysteries of the cosmos. So it's ironic to note that this technological marvel had an embarrassingly modest startup.

The first images Hubble sent back to Earth were not the ones that made history. They were blurred. Some technicians had mistakenly dropped some washers costing twenty-five cents apiece into the magnificent machine's optical testing device, but no one at NASA knew it until the Hubble was hovering in orbit.

The ultimate price tag for repairs was $86 million. It would have been only $2 million had the difficulties been found before blastoff.

79

WATERWORLD:
ALL WET FROM
THE BEGINNING

T he most frightening horror stories from Hollywood almost never come from the imaginations of script-writers. They more often recount real-life tales of terror about movies that never live up to their artistic or financial expectations and why those films fail so utterly. Almost invariably, these sagas wind up describing some breathtaking idiocies that could only happen in the land of the silver screen.

Kevin Costner's summer 1995 whale of a flop, *Waterworld*, for example, was shot in the open sea off Hawaii for maximum verisimilitude. This crafty decision played a big role in extending filming to 166 days and ballooning its budget to record proportions.

There was lots of reshooting to do for scenes that were ruined by such things as boats on the horizon. In the post-apocalypse setting of this sci-fi dud, such things were not supposed to exist. There was also the problem of crew days lost to seasickness and gouging by local merchants with a captive-market film crew to rip off.

These and other problems like sinking sets, high winds, and a script-in-progress approach to filmmaking helped drive the production costs for the movie to, well, in Hollywood, where the creative accountants dwell, you never really know, but $175 million was a nice round number. Some estimates were higher. No one was denying that *Waterworld* was, to date, the most expensive movie of all time.

All of which meant that to earn any kind of reasonable profit, *Waterworld* would have to have strong legs in movie theaters, video sales and rentals, foreign exhibition, cable and broadcast television, merchandising, and other rights.

The film debuted to mixed reviews at best, with some zingers that really hurt. Why, some wondered, was everyone always so filthy when they inhabited a world with virtually no dry land in it? How did mutation happen to leave the hero played by Kevin Kostner with webbed feet but not webbed hands? And if everyone's living on the water in bright sun, how come there's only one character with a tan?

Despite a buoyant opening weekend gross of more than $20 million, *Waterworld* wound up sinking fast at the box office and was all wet as a profit maker for MCA.

80

AMAZON PULPS
PAPER PLAN

The barges were too big for the Panama Canal, so they had to go around Africa from Japan to get to the Amazon basin. They carried some stupendous equipment: a giant pulp mill and paper plant.

The machinery was twenty stories high and weighed sixty-six thousand tons. It was headed deep into the Brazilian interior where it would be set up to make the next billion-dollar fortune for entrepreneur Daniel K. Ludwig.

It was the late 1960s, and Ludwig foresaw a coming paper shortage as the world moved into the computer age. Ludwig was a billionaire who had made earlier fortunes by correctly anticipating trends in shipping, mining, oil, ranching, and gambling. His paper plan involved the purchase of a Connecticut-size parcel of land along the Jari River in the Amazon basin.

In the late 1970s, the huge pulp mill and paper plant

were floated to a site that had been cleared by thirty-five thousand workers and planted with pine and eucalyptus trees that botanists said were right for the difficult environment. Ludwig's plan—to go from plant to paper in the tropics of Brazil—seemed a masterstroke. So what if no one had been able to conquer the difficult Amazon environment before? The march of progress was unstoppable, wasn't it?

No one could ever say that Ludwig didn't give it his best. He lost an estimated billion dollars of his personal fortune in the attempt to make the Amazon basin flow with paper. But not even Daniel Ludwig's gargantuan bank account and infrastructure could overcome the little things about doing business in the Amazon that everyone knew about and had inhibited success before.

There were leaf cutter ants that ravaged crops and supplies. There were malaria and meningitis-carrying insects that spread disease and infection among Ludwig's workforce. The sparse soil of the region couldn't support Ludwig's trees.

Daniel K. Ludwig wasn't the first to think he could beat the jungle, but no one has ever lost more trying.

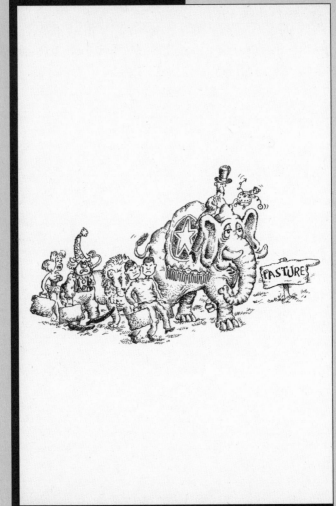

BARNUM GOES BELLY UP

81

No Winning Place
for a Showman

P. T. Barnum was one of the great showmen. His capacity to understand what people wanted in entertainment helped the Barnum & Bailey Circus more than live up to its immodest slogan, The Greatest Show on Earth. Barnum brought attractions that capitalized on people's unslakable thirst for the unusual and even the grotesque. There was Tom Thumb, the midget general. Chang and Eng were Siamese twins. Jumbo was a huge African elephant. It was a nonstop parade of can-you-top-this oddities.

But Barnum's showbiz brilliance didn't translate into investing savvy. The man who had no trouble seeing how to amuse the masses had terrible trouble spotting good investments.

His worst was probably the Jerome Clock Company. Barnum chalked up a $500,000 loss in the untimely venture, and wound up bankrupt as a result.

82

How Orange County Got Peeled

The people who live in Orange County, California, are, by and large, well-heeled and conservative. They live in tony towns like Newport Beach or San Clemente, and generally tend to believe that the government that governs least governs best. It's a Republican place where the idea is to keep services high and taxes low. It's also where you find Disneyland.

This mix of money, marketism, and magical thinking boiled over in December 1994 when Orange County declared the largest municipal bankruptcy in American municipal history. County officials had lost more than $1.5 billion gambling on the direction of interest rates with securities that are known as "derivatives." These high-risk pieces of paper are so complicated that even the professionals who trade them are often not really sure what they're buying and selling.

In Orange County, treasurer Robert Citron had been

playing with fire, but winning. His strategy had returned high rewards, and nobody was asking too many questions about whether his investments were prudent when things were going well.

In fact, an investigation of the financial debacle ultimately revealed that Orange County had been living beyond its means, using the proceeds from its derivative investing to stay ahead of the game instead of investing more prudently and shifting some of the revenue burden to its residents.

Why had Orange County's public servants chosen gambling over a tax increase? As we mentioned, Orange County is a Republican place where they like services high and their taxes low.

In the end, it was disclosed that Citron, who pleaded guilty to some fraud charges, had actually involved astrologers and psychics in his money management.

The citizens of Orange County had gotten what they paid for.

SOME THINGS DON'T GO BETTER WITH COKE

83

Coke with Film: A Bad Taste

Coca-Cola and the movies have been going around together since the first film went through sprockets. Coke was an integral part of show biz. In 1982, the top minds at the top soft drink company decided that it was time for Coke to own the movies. Coke acquired Columbia Pictures for $750 million.

Long before the deal was done, there were those who said Coke had gone soft in the head. You can't make and market movies like Coca-Cola, said the naysayers. Nonsense was the word from Atlanta, where Coke keeps its world headquarters.

From the start, it was a bad marriage. The folks from Coke who came in to call the shots mixed with the Columbia brass like Coke and film. Decisions to cut costs and increase film production left shortfalls in marketing budgets. Consumer surveys to pick winning plots and bankable stars couldn't stop some of the worst movies of all time from being made. You might remember *Ish-tar*, a $40 million mess from Elaine May that not even Warren Beatty and Dustin Hoffman would carry to profits.

The critics were right, you can't make and sell movies like soft drinks. Hollywood had burned Atlanta before, but it was only let's pretend in the 1930s classic film *Gone With the Wind.* The Columbia debacle for Coke was the real thing.

84

Jingo Blows:
Those Ugly American
Names

What's in a name?

Plenty, as lots of American companies have found out when they have tried to sell their products abroad. From McDonald's to General Motors, there have been some big-time bungles in attempts to translate the stateside nomenclature of success into international sales. Attempts at using the American name on a product marketed outside the U.S. have created some truly jaw-dropping jocularity.

You have to wonder why nobody at GM seemed to understand that the name Nova, a Chevy compact car, sounds like the words "it doesn't go" in Spanish. And where were the watchdogs at Ford who might have warned that the name of its compact, Pinto, was slang for "small penis" in Brazil?

The meaning of Pledge in Dutch has nothing to do with promises. It means "piss," as the chagrined folks at Johnson's Wax found out when they sold the furniture polish in The Netherlands under its American name. And what kind of establishments do you suppose the French thought McDonald's was running when the golden arches appeared on the Champs Élysées with a Big Mac sandwich on the menu that translates indelicately into French as "big pimp."

85

HUNTING FOR A SILVER LINING

Their father claimed he had a "genius gene," but it seems H. L. Hunt didn't pass it along to his sons Herbert and Bunker.

The Hunt boys were big players in the silver market in the early 1970s, shortly before the death of their oil tycoon father. They did so well that they decided to try to corner the market. By the end of the 1970s, the Hunt brothers owned 130 million ounces of silver, with contracts to buy 90 million more. Inflation, the Hunt's buying spree, and world tensions from the Soviet Union's invasion of Afghanistan drove silver prices up to $50 an ounce by the beginning of 1980, far above the Hunt brothers' average price per ounce.

It was the best of times for Herbert and Bunker Hunt. Their strategy had brought them billions, but the profits were still on paper. The Hunt brothers were holding out for higher prices. They were about to learn the lasting truth of the old investing adage that "pigs eat, but hogs get slaughtered."

The market the Hunts were busy cornering had a player named Uncle Sam who would ultimately do them in. Uneasy with what was happening in silver, the federal government exercised its regulatory powers and threw the market for a loop by limiting speculation in silver futures. Prices tanked, dropping all the way to $21 an ounce in only three months. With the waterfall drop came huge margin calls on the Hunt brothers, requiring them to come up with as much as $10 million a day in cash to meet their obligations.

They were rich, but not that rich. Not even a $1.1 billion loan from Uncle Sam could keep the Hunts from bankruptcy. By 1990, the high-flying billionaire Hunts, who had also lost big when oil prices tumbled in the 1980s, saw their personal fortunes shrink to less than $2 million each.

Despite their financial trauma, the descendants of the self-proclaimed genius gene–carrier were tough to feel sorry for.

86

MINIVAN, MAXIWINNER

Imitation, they say, is the sincerest form of flattery. In some cases, it might also be suggested that imitation is also an admission of initial idiocy. Could this be said of Ford and Chevrolet in the case of the minivan?

The snickers were virtually audible when Chrysler put it around that it would attempt to make minivans the replacement for that time-honored American family carrier, the station wagon. The loudest laughs were heard where station wagon market shares were highest, at Ford and Chevy.

But those smiles quickly changed to gasps when the 1984 model year rolled around, and Chrysler's front-wheel-drive Dodge Caravan and Plymouth Voyager minivans made the scene. The new vehicles were an instant success, going on in years to come to dominate 50 percent of the minivan market they had created.

Ford and Chevy had their own minivans on the market within a year, but there was no denying that they had been caught with their fenders down.

87

FEDEX OUTFAXED

It seems hard to believe in the age of E-mail, but Federal Express once thought it could build a major new profit center by selling fax machine services to businesses. The company that specialized in getting packages and documents to customers when they absolutely positively had to be there overnight was now going to deliver documents even faster.

The year was 1984 and the optimism at FedEx was high. Under its system, called ZapMail, FedEx would pick up a document, hurry it down to a nearby FedEx office, fax it to a FedEx office in the city of the intended recipient, and deliver it to the appropriate address.

Really big customers would have a FedEx ZapMailer that would send documents via satellite to other places where ZapMailers had been installed.

FedEx spent hundreds of millions on a satellite system for document transmission and gave ZapMail an extensive two-year tryout to break into the black. But the timing that had looked so right for the diversification turned out to be wrong. Businesses were buying their own fax machines, which proved to be a more economical option than ZapMail. There were also technical problems with the ZapMail network that wound up creating too many transmission errors.

After two years and more than $230 million in losses, FedEx zapped its ZapMail. America *had* fallen in love with the fax, and the cold facts for FedEx were that its attempt to win the business couldn't cut it.

88

High-Tech Jail
Is a Bust

The new detention center in Baltimore County, Maryland, was billed as the most modern jail in the U.S. when it was ready for its first inmates in 1982. It had solar heating, surveillance cameras everywhere, unbreakable windows, computers to control everything, and an $11.2 million price tag.

It soon became apparent that "most modern" didn't mean best, at all. Baltimore taxpayers had been tagged with a doozy of a mess. The remote control cameras worked beautifully, as long as you didn't need good functioning for more than thirty minutes. After that, their motors burned out. Locks sprang open and microphones used to speak to prisoners didn't work. Those avant-garde solar panels froze in the winter.

The sightlines from guard posts made it hard to see prisoners on the cellblock, and the computers sometimes locked up the guards by trapping them in various parts of the building.

Before a year had gone by, nine prisoners escaped from the allegedly break-proof jailhouse.

They kicked out the unbreakable windows.

89

HEAVEN'S GATE:
NO SALVATION

Many Hollywood movies fail, but none had ever failed this spectacularly. Director Michael Cimino's 1980 mistake fest, *Heaven's Gate,* was the ultimate movie from hell.

It was not supposed to have been. Cimino was riding high. His Vietnam film, *The Deer Hunter,* had won five Oscars, and made him the man of the moment in Hollywood. But the acclaimed *"auteur"* became *"quel horreur."*

Cimino's ego knew no bounds on the *Heaven's Gate* production, and none was set by his financiers, United Artists. The film ran over its $11.5 million budget by some $33 million, making it the most expensive film ever shot at the time. This was quite an achievement for a Western with no high-salaried stars or budget-busting special effects.

Cimino achieved this dubious distinction by shooting

one and a half million feet of film, fifteen times the normal amount of celluloid exposed. He ordered full crews to be on call as much as eighteen hours a day, seven days a week, so that no flash of his creative genius would go unrecorded. He ordered sets to be torn down and rebuilt.

Cimino's girlfriend kept track of the spending. With virtually no Hollywood experience, she had been given the job of line producer on the production.

Without traditional creative or financial oversight, United Artists was betting on Cimino's artistic vision to bring in the bucks. All it brought in was the boos.

After five hundred hours of editing, the *auteur* produced an interminable three-hour-and-thirty-nine-minute dud that critics immediately hounded back into the edit room for a recut. One writer called it the kind of film "you want to deface by drawing a mustache on it." A revised two-hour-and-twenty-four-minute version wasn't the answer to commercial success.

The mistake on *Heaven's Gate* turned out to be the end of United Artists as an independent company. It went out of business and was eventually bought by MGM. To the end, Cimino maintained the trouble with his work of art was the audience's lack of sophistication.

90

THE SCARLET LETTER: A IS FOR AWFUL

The A that Hester Prynne had to wear on her breast branded her an adulteress in the famous novel by Nathaniel Hawthorne, *The Scarlet Letter*.

The As the 1995 film racked up had lots of different meanings. The critics said the movie was (starts with "a") awful, making movie fans wonder why anyone thought the cinematic trip through the American classic was necessary in the first place.

It was a rough ride for a novel that didn't lend itself to a facile translation to a new medium. The movie went through an (starts with "a") astounding twenty-five re-writes of its story, and three different endings were created. Some of the brilliant additions to the original Hawthorne included the ingenious idea of taking leading lady Demi Moore out of her clothes and putting her into a bath.

But not even the delicious Demi in the buff could bring in (starts with "a") audiences. Moore was less at the box office. The film's scarlet letter turned out to be F—fifty-million-dollar flop.

TIPPLES NOT INCLUDED

The bean counters at Pan Am were worried that flight attendants might be making off with some of those little bottles of liquor. After all, their job descriptions specified that tipples were not included.

Pan Am rigged planes with security devices that had special mechanisms to monitor the opening and closing of liquor cabinet doors. Nobody told the Pan Am people in the planes, since they were the ones under suspicion.

One stewardess thought the new contraption in the cabinet looked suspicious, and might be a bomb. She told the pilot, and he made an emergency landing. All of the plane's eighty passengers were forced to get off through emergency exits.

We don't know if complimentary drinks were served to make up for the passengers' inconvenience.

WHEN THEY PUBLISHED,
IT PERISHED

The company published *Time, Fortune, Sports Illus-trated, Money,* and other famous and profitable magazines. But Time, Inc. missed the mark badly in the mid-1980s with a publication named *TV-Cable Week.*

Plans called for the new magazine to provide listings of broadcast and cable television programming mixed with the top-quality writing and reporting that made the company's established magazines leaders in their fields. Cable TV systems would sell the product to their subscribers.

Even though the distribution idea was untried before, and there were other places people could find out what was on television, *TV-Cable Week* was much ballyhooed in magazine circles. Time, Inc. executives boldly pre-dicted quick success for the venture, suggesting that the new product would eventually outsell even *Time*, the company's flagship publication.

But the bravado broke down when *TV-Cable Week* failed to perform. Cable system operators were poor at marketing. The editorial product broke no new ground. The magazine that had kindled such hopes high up at Time, Inc. got a relative ho-hum from readers.

In one of the fastest and most expensive exits in magazine publishing history, Time, Inc. put the putative heir apparent to *Time* out of business after only six months in the marketplace, admitting to losses of $47 million on *TV-Cable Week*.

"M-O-N-E-Y": Ovitz Leaves Disney

93

OVITZ EXITS

Business and friendship don't mix. It's a time-honored truth. But sometimes the most simple truths are lost on the brightest people.

What other explanation can there be for the show business personnel bungle of the century that Disney boss Michael Eisner made by inviting his good super-agent friend Michael Ovitz into the mouse kingdom to be his number two?

Ovitz had built the Creative Artists Agency into a powerhouse, earning himself a reputation as Hollywood's most powerful man in the process. How would he ever be able park his ego and accept a subordinate post under Eisner? No problem, said Eisner, he and Ovitz would operate more as partners.

How would Ovitz, a deal maker with no operating experience, do as an executive?

The answer was in after little more than a year. Disney's duumvirate of Eisner and Ovitz was kaput, and Ovitz was out faster than you could say "bibbity bobbity boo."

It was an odd couple from the start, but nobody really got hurt. Eisner admitted to a momentary lapse of judgment and went back to running the Disney empire. Ovitz cut a sweetheart deal of $90 million in cash and stock in severance for fourteen months of work and went off to plan his next move.

It all seemed to prove another time-honored truth that in Hollywood the greatest talent is the ability to fail forward.

94

EuroDisney: Discontent on the Continent

It was built on land that was used for growing sugar beets, so the creators of the EuroDisney theme park outside Paris had some reason to hope for sweet results. But almost from the start, the American cultural transplant went on the critical list.

EuroDisneyland opened into the teeth of a European recession in the early 1990s, and it had to fight a weak dollar and some negative tweaks from French intellectuals which hurt attendance. The weak dollar made it cheaper for Europeans to come to America to see the original Disney attractions. The French intellectuals attacked the land of Mickey Mouse as a "Trojan horse of American culture."

Many early doubters of Disney's designs in Europe said "I told you so."

The $4 billion project was soon running deeply in the red and facing a possible bankruptcy. Disney pumped in $1 million to keep the park afloat and ultimately a deal with sixty banks averted the crisis.

But the first French experience had long since wiped the smile off Mickey's mouth.

95

AMERICAN EXPRESS:
NOT TO ITS CREDIT

In its advertising, American Express has long sought to build an image of itself as a company with integrity that you can trust and always rely on. Which is why the stories about its alleged attempt to smear a competitor did so much damage to the credit card company's carefully crafted reputation. Had people at American Express somehow gone daft?

The reports in question painted a portrait of seamy corporate intrigue designed to trash the reputation of a high-profile international banker named Edmond J. Safra. A publicity-shunning man, Safra had sold his Swiss private banking business to Amex in the 1980s and stayed on to run it.

Quickly, it became apparent that Safra's style and the way American Express wanted to do business were a bad mix, and Safra resigned his banking post with the company in 1984, agreeing not to go back into banking competition with American Express until 1988.

Though he was gone, he was hardly forgotten in the corridors and offices of American Express, and eventually there were charges that the company mounted an international effort to sully Safra's reputation by promoting newspaper and other stories seeking to link Safra to drug smuggling, money laundering, and illegal arms dealing.

How could one man strike such fear into a company with the reputation and resources of American Express? All the facts will never be known. Amex never laid out the chapter and verse about what happened and never admitted explicit wrongdoing, but the company ultimately did issue a written apology to Safra and paid $8 million to the banker's favorite charities.

In a written statement about the affair, American Express did use the word "shameful" in describing the effort against Safra's reputation. It was a word many also used to describe American Express for a long time after the Safra situation came to light.

96

SOUR NOTES
FROM CBS IN MUSIC

CBS wanted to be a player in the musical instrument business, but its strategy was out of tune with intelligent business methods.

The "Tiffany" network bought into the music biz in the mid-1960s with the acquisition of Fender Musical Instruments, a maker of guitars, amplifiers, and other items designed to create sensational sounds.

Buyouts of some other household names in instrumentation followed. These included Steinway & Sons, the legendary piano maker, and other companies that made flutes, harps, organs, and speakers.

Industry observers noted that CBS paid high prices for these acquisitions, and then demanded unrealistic rates of return from their managements. Big bucks were spent on bad ideas, like a lavish corporate headquarters outside Chicago.

It was a formula for losing money that worked beautifully. By the mid-1980s, losses had totaled more than $40 million, and CBS decided to get out of the musical instrument business by selling off the companies it had acquired.

97

The Money Giving Game

of

Egos and Inches

Government and big business belt tightening in the 1990s has put an increasing emphasis on the contributions of philanthropists to pay for things that governments and corporations used to. It's part of a new way of doing business in the American system that's been controversial but often quite effective.

The double-take-inducing headline that greeted readers of *The New York Times* one May morning in 1997 indicated that there were still plenty of kinks in the system. It read: "$3 MILLION ZOO GIFT REVOKED BECAUSE PLAQUE IS TOO SMALL."

It seemed hard to believe, but Edith and Henry Everett, two of the New York City's most generous philanthropists, were apparently taking back their gift to rebuild the charming Children's Zoo in Central Park because the size of the letters on a plaque to commemorate their graciousness was too small. It seemed that the letters in question were only to be two inches high. The Everetts weren't even getting an inch for each million.

It also stuck in the unhappy former donor's craw that their names would be sharing billing at the rebuilt zoo with the original nice people who had put up the dough to build the children's fantasyland in the first place, former New York Governor Herbert H. Lehman and his wife, Edith.

The Everetts put the onus for their decision on the New York City Art Commission, whose unacceptable word on plaques was the letter of the law. The art commission said it didn't really have a heart of stone, it was just that the zoo was a part of New York history, and it felt the names of earlier benefactors also deserved a place.

And where, you might ask, was the thinking about the children in this melee of misplaced priorities? On a May morning in New York City in 1997, it looked like the interests of the youngsters for whose pleasure the whole zoo project was undertaken in the first place had become lost in an idiotic battle of egos and inches that sometimes comes with the territory in the big business game of money giving.

But appearances are often deceiving and the future of the Children's Zoo was finally secured when the Tisch Foundation, headed by Laurence Tisch and his brother, Preston Robert Tisch, agreed after the Everetts withdrew their gift to replace the donation and add up to $1.5 million more. And how do they want their gift of $4.5 million to be acknowledged? "I couldn't care less what they do," said Laurence Tisch.

230

98

THE SCUTTLING
OF SCULLEY

If you went looking for the prime example of a corporate statesman, you would have had trouble topping John Sculley, the chairman of Apple Computer in 1993. The former Pepsico exec was personable, articulate, telegenic, and mentioned regularly as a prime contender for a top government job or bigger things in corporate America.

Then one day, Sculley announced he was resigning from Apple to take the helm at Spectrum Information Technologies.

Spectrum Information Technologies?

Few people had heard of the tiny Long Island company and those who had were not impressed. Spectrum was in the wireless technology business, but its track record was spotty. The company was very small. It wasn't profitable. What was Sculley doing?

Because of who he was, it was assumed that Sculley

knew where he was going and what he was doing. People like John Sculley always do their homework, don't they?

It turned out that whatever homework on Spectrum Sculley might have done, he had come up with the wrong answers and trashed one of the highest-profile careers in American business in the process. In four months, Sculley had quit Spectrum and was suing the company's president for fraud. Spectrum countersued for breach of contract. In the crossfire, everyone learned just how credulous Sculley had been in choosing his new employer. Eventually the lawsuits were dropped but the self-inflicted damage to Sculley's reputation had been done.

99

THESE JOANS WERE ARCH

J oan Collins is better known for the turn of her ankle than her ability to turn a phrase, but that didn't stop Joni Evans at Random House from giving the actress a contract to write two novels and a $1.2 million advance to do the job in the mid-1990s.

Collins did turn in two books. They were entitled *The Ruling Passion* and *Hell Hath No Fury*. The plots followed two sisters—one blond and beautiful, the other dark and ugly—from bed to bed. Other details of the two stories were less interesting and a lot less clear. The plots were so mixed up that Collins herself had trouble recalling who was doing what to whom. The sisters suffer life-threatening diseases, for instance, but the maladies affecting them switch from sibling to sibling.

Joni Evans was not amused, labeling the work by Joan Collins jumbled, disjointed, and unpublishable. Random House went to court to get its money back.

But Collins's agent, the deft publishing player Irving "Swifty" Lazar, had managed to negotiate a customary "satisfactory performance" clause out of the deal Collins had signed. So the actress, who had handed in two complete manuscripts, had to be paid for them, even if they were completely awful.

THEY MADE A LIST,
BUT DIDN'T CHECK IT TWICE

Long-distance phone companies are always battling for customers, and they've come up with lots of creative ways to get people to switch long-distance carriers. One of the more effective techniques is sending a check to people that switches their phone service when they cash the check from the phone company that sent it.

That's what AT&T thought it was doing when it sent a batch of checks for $50 to a mailing list in the mid-1990s.

But it turned out that the people on the list already used AT&T long distance.

Rather than cancel the checks, AT&T let the recipients cash them.

THE N(o) B(rains) A(pparent) Knicks

The superstars of modern professional basketball earn more money than most corporate chief executives. Their single-game salaries surpass the yearly takes of most American workers.

It's tempting to think of these jocks as sportsmen, but they are, in fact, entertainment industry businessmen whose individual profit margins are directly related to their personal statistics and team achievements. When their teams win championships, their personal stocks go up.

These are the unwritten rules of the big-time basketball game, and the men who play in the NBA know them by heart. But they aren't the only rules that these folks with the oversized bodies and sometimes undersized intellects need to live by on the job.

The league has a written code that unambiguously sets the limits of conduct on the court. The relevant language from NBA Rule 12 says: "During an altercation, all players not taking part in the game must remain in the immediate vicinity of the bench. Violators will be suspended without pay for a minimum of one game and fined up to $25,000."

With this language buried somewhere in their brains, four of the most important cogs in the 1997 New York Knicks' drive for a long-sought NBA championship raced off the bench at the end of an already-lost conference semifinal playoff game in Miami to join a fight that erupted when a large Miami Heat player flipped a small Knick after a free throw.

The four important cogs were

- center Patrick Ewing, a perennial all-star and the team's leading scorer
- guard Allan Houston, a hot-shooting high-paid 1997 Knick addition and the team's second leading scorer
- forward Larry Johnson, another big bucks starter and key contributor
- guard John Starks, winner of the NBA's best "sixth man" award and a key reserve

The NBA immediately suspended the four, along with several other players including the Miami flipper and the Knick flippee, for one playoff game, as its clearly written rule demanded. It was the strongest disciplinary action the NBA had ever taken during its playoffs.

The episode instantly transformed an easy Knick canter into the conference finals against Michael Jordan and the Chicago Bulls into an unnecessary forced march. The Knicks would now have to attempt to win the best of seven series—which it led after the game with the bench-clearing fight by three games to two—without its most potent players.

It was too much for the Knicks to overcome. New York lost games six and seven, and went home for the summer. The Miami Heat, whose players had kept their heads and stayed on the bench, moved on to challenge the Michael Jordan et al.

And so it was that a group of America's most highly paid businessmen sabotaged their pursuit of a cherished long-term goal with a collective dumb decision in the heat of battle. Messrs. Ewing, Houston, Johnson, and Starks didn't describe their momentary lapse of reason that way, but that was pretty much the bottom line.